Green and Pleasant Land

Steve Humphries & Beverley Hopwood

Green and Pleasant Land

First published 1999 by Channel 4 Books, an imprint of Macmillan Publishers Ltd
25 Eccleston Place, London SW1W 9NF, Basingstoke and Oxford

www.macmillan.co.uk

ISBN 0 7522 1784 4

Design by Production Line
Colour reproduction by Speedscan
Printed and bound in Italy by New Interlitho

This book accompanies the television series *Green and Pleasant Land* made by Testimony Films for Channel 4.
Executive producer: Angela Holdsworth
Producer: Steve Humphries

Picture Acknowledgements

Gordon Anderson: 29; Ruth Armstrong: 94; Marian Atkinson: 99; Beaford Archive: 31, 72;
Beamish Regional Resource Centre Photographic Library: 14, 16, 28, 77, 101; Joyce Bennett: 102, 103;
Florence Bowley: 82; Dartington Rural Archive: 74; Edinburgh City Libraries: 37; Lady Maureen Fellowes: 59;
Garland Collection, West Sussex Record Office: 75, 96, 114, 124; Howarth-Loomes: 90; Hulton Getty: half title,
half title verso, 5, 8–9, 10, 17, 26, 39, 41, 43, 44, 45, 47, 48, 51, 56, 60–1, 64–5, 67, 68, 78, 81, 83, 84, 86, 89, 107,
111, 112, 116, 130, 134, 138, 144, 145, 146, 147, 148, 149, 150, 155, 162, 165, 166–7, 169, 171; Albert Gillett: 34;
Con Gray: 15; Imperial War Museum: 141; Keele University Library: 52; Sybil Marshall: 153; Ed Mitchell: 36;
Norman Mursell: 46, 70, 71; Popperfoto: 106, 142; Cyril Rice: 55; Marjorie Riddaway: 24, 151; Joan Rogers: 132;
Mary Rowling: 92; Museum of Rural Life: 20, 33, 38, 109, 115, 121, 123, 139, 156, 164, 172, 174;
School of Scottish Studies, University of Edinburgh: 128–9; Scottish Life Archive: 21, 27, 80, 93, 97,
118, 127; David Spreckley: 69, 105; Dot Stephenson: 161; Suffolk Photographic Survey: 119;
Associated Press/Topham Picturepoint: 159; Topham Picturepoint 12, 23, 110, 126, 136;
John Waspe: 120; Welsh Folk Museum: 19.

Contents

Acknowledgements

We would like to thank all the people who have helped us in writing this book and making the television series it accompanies, with special thanks to Peter Grimsdale and Michael Jackson for backing the project. Thanks also to Gill Brown of Channel 4, executive producer Angela Holdsworth and consultants Paul Thompson, Stephen Hussey, Jacque Sarsby and Doc Rowe for their valuable contribution. And thanks to Sue Shepherd and Joanna Mack for their input into this project when it was first conceived ten years ago.

We are grateful to the Testimony Films team, especially to Andy Attenburrow and Daniel de Waal, and to the principal series researchers Hilary Jelbert and Mary Parsons. Also thanks to photograph and film researcher Richard van Emden, associate producer Miriam Akhtar, production secretary Madge Reed, production manager Mike Humphries, cameramen Steve Haskett and Mike Pharey and sound recordists Jeff John, Tony Brown and David Harcombe. Thanks for additional help with research to Anna Gore-Langton, Lucy Swingler, Katherine Nightingale, Yvette Staelens, Jeffrey Olstead, Carolyn Schagen, Wendy Nelson, Jane Rugman, Gill Hennessey, Amanda Kennett, Gill Powell, Kate Spiers, Alan Golding, John Eldridge, Carol Trewin, Rob Perks, Phil Gardner, Joan Mant, Marilyn Davies, Mark Hopwood and Anne Marie-Hughes.

For their advice and support we are grateful to Alison Shipley, Jan Faull and the staff of the National Film and Television Archive, The Museum of Rural Life at the University of Reading, Bristol Central Library and the BBC Bristol Library.

Finally and most importantly, we wish to thank all the contributors to this project who told us their stories and kindly lent us their photographs.

Introduction

Life in the British countryside has, in the twentieth century, changed out of all recognition. Oak Apple Day, St. Valentine's Day and Pig Killing Day have long ceased to be the highlights of the country child's year. Farm hands no longer pour into the local market town for the hiring fair. Today, harvest celebrations are only a faint echo of the communal feasting and festivities of days gone by.

The age of horse power on the farm, when horses pulled everything from ploughs to muck carts, has gone forever. The small mixed farms that once formed the backbone of the rural economy have largely been replaced as a result of a second agricultural revolution that has vastly increased the size and productivity of land holdings. In the 1900s, more than one in ten of all British men worked in agriculture. Today it is less than one in a hundred. And the old village, once a bustling working community living off the land, has now become a fashionable middle-class enclave.

The old rural world still survives, however, in the memories of the men and women who lived and worked in the countryside during the first decades of the twentieth century. Their lives, shaped by local custom and traditional ideas, seem closer to the seventeenth century than to a post-modern industrial society on the cusp of the new millennium. The aim of this book, and the television series it accompanies, has been to capture the stories of those people who can still recall the time-honoured rural way of life before it vanishes forever.

The British countryside, our 'green and pleasant land', holds a special place in our affections. The old village life has for generations been regarded as embracing the best of our national character. It forms a central place in our sense of history and national identity. Its values have appeared strong and stable in an ever-changing, restless and superficial industrial world. There is a huge and growing nostalgia industry of autobiographies, picture books, popular histories and museums that paint a charming and rosy picture of our rural past. These images of a rural idyll with chocolate-box villages and salt of the earth country yokels have fuelled the gentrification of the countryside by the middle classes.

The May Day hobby-horse parade was a custom which survived in some villages into the twentieth century.

While recognizing the appeal and the attractions of the world we have lost, it has not been our intention to romanticize the old farms and villages. We have endeavoured to delve beneath this to discover the realities – sometimes harsh and brutal – of life in old rural Britain.

There was a darker side, which has often been overlooked, to the centuries-old country traditions. During the first decades of the century this took the form of child labour, semi-feudal tyranny, narrow social and sexual mores,

exploitation by farmers who paid some of the lowest wages in Britain and a frequent absence of facilities, such as running water and sanitation. And perhaps one of the most neglected facts about life in the pre-war countryside was the grinding poverty of many who lived there.

This is not, however, the story of downtrodden country people. What is most striking about the testimonies we feature is the dignity, determination, good humour, creativity, resourcefulness and sheer hard graft displayed, often in the face of the most difficult and demanding circumstances.

In writing the book, we have collected stories from more than one and a half thousand people, most of them born in the period from the 1900s to 1920s. Many wrote to us about their memories in answer to our call published in country newspapers all over Britain. Most of the voices heard in the book are those of around fifty people whom we interviewed in depth and filmed for the television series. They were chosen because of the vividness of their memories and their ability to illustrate a broad spectrum of experience of the country. Here they tell their own stories in their own words, sometimes for the first time. We hear the voice of some of our oldest country folk: agricultural labourers and farmers, poachers and gamekeepers, aristocrats and servants, mothers who bore and brought up some of the largest families in Britain, the stigmatized single parent with her 'bastard' child and the villagers who bore the brunt of the air bombardment during the Second World War.

Each of the six chapters explores a key theme in country life and the development of rural Britain. The first five chapters begin with a historical introduction, sketching the background to the testimonies that follow. They feature country childhood, life on the semi-feudal estates, sexual behaviour, farm life in the years of the agricultural depression, and the countryside during the Second World War. The final chapter describes the social revolution of the post-war years that changed rural Britain forever.

In this book we have documented the authentic voice of country people from the top to the bottom of the social scale. It has been fascinating to meet and talk to so many of our oldest countrymen and women. Those we feature were very open in their responses and refreshingly honest, revealing some of their most intimate stories. We hope we have done them justice.

– One –

Lost Childhood

Children join hands
before dancing
around the bonfire
in a Northumbrian
village in the 1900s.
Afterwards, the
villagers would
scatter sweets
for them.

For children living in the Somerset village of Chalfont St. Peter in the 1920s and 1930s, the last Thursday in October was the most important day of the year – Punkie Night. They would parade from one cottage to the next, knocking on doors brandishing their punkies – scooped-out mangolds (a kind of beet), carefully carved with an eerie face and containing a lighted candle. Then they would sing the Punkie song, as Mavis Pippin, now aged seventy-eight, still vividly remembers:

'Punkie Night was as special to us as Christmas, perhaps even more so. We went to every house in the village, especially the big ones, because they had more money and we'd sing our Punkie song. It went:

It's Punkie Night tonight, it's Punkie Night tonight,
Give us a candle, give us a light, it's Punkie Night tonight.
It's Punkie Night tonight, it's Punkie Night tonight,
Adam and Eve they wouldn't believe, it's Punkie Night tonight.

'We did sing that with all our might and they'd come out and give us a few pennies. That was wonderful to us, we'd keep that for sweets.'

Punkie Night was one of a host of village children's calendar customs, many of them unique to their own locality. They often involved begging, dressing up and making mischief. The most widely celebrated were Valentine's Day (14 February), April Fool's Day (1 April), May Day (1 May) and Oak Apple Day (29 May). In the North Devon village of Atherington there was even a spring-time Stinging Nettle Day. One of the girls who brandished nettles in the school playground was Marjorie Riddaway, now aged 91.

'Once a year we had Nettle Day, but what it signified I'll never know. It would start early in the morning on the way to school and we'd all pick the longest stinging nettle we could find, hold it with an old piece of rag and sting whoever we could. And that continued all day at playtime and after school. 'Twas cruel really and the teachers would try and shelter some of the children but you couldn't get far away from it because everyone was doing it and enjoying it too. Mind you it could be very painful, the sting was dreadfully strong. You'd have to spit on it and rub it with a dock leaf. It was great fun.'

In a modern world of play dominated by television, computer games, and widespread paranoia of the paedophile, the rural childhood of an older generation can appear like a kind of Paradise Lost. In many ways there was a great sense of freedom. During the first decades of the century village children had few toys, but they enjoyed more natural, and perhaps more innocent, pursuits like climbing trees, damming streams and playing hide-and-seek in the woods. Instead of bought toys there were 'found objects', such as tree branches which could be shaped into all manner of rough-and-ready cricket bats, boats and fishing rods.

Many autobiographies, such as Flora Thompson's *Lark Rise to Candelford* and Laurie Lee's *Cider with Rosie* celebrate the richness and spontaneity of children's play in the unspoilt countryside of old England. The migration to the cities and decades of agricultural depression had left a picturesque landscape with many a ruined barn and rambling hedge where children could play. The countryside became in children's eyes a great adventure playground where their imagination could run wild. Since most of their activities were outdoors and made use of nature's bounty, the games were often seasonal. There were skating and snowballing in winter, looking for birds' eggs in the spring, swimming in the summer and conkers in the autumn.

Boys fishing in the River Darent in Shoreham, Kent in the 1920s.

Much of the time the country child was a hunter-gatherer. In the fields and hedgerows there was an abundance of food for free: wild strawberries, hawthorn berries, nuts, blackberries, wild mushrooms and apples were some of the most popular. Most would be eaten raw, though some were taken back for Mother to turn into delicious pies, jams and jellies. For the poorest the food helped fill an empty stomach. Some of the fruit and vegetables would be pilfered from farmers' fields, often on the way home from school in the late afternoon. Although this was a criminal offence very few were detected or prosecuted by the village policeman. In the cases where the farmer discovered children pilfering from his fields the most likely outcome was a warning to the parents. The country child usually escaped detection anyway, as most knew the lie of the land; they were also quick-witted and could outrun their elders and betters.

Their hunting skills were really put to the test in catching rabbits, of which there was an abundant supply. Using nets, ferrets, sticks and catapults, children killed many a rabbit for the pot – usually gratefully received by the parents. Rabbit was a crucial part of the diet before the Second World War and often the only meat eaten on a regular basis by the agricultural labourer and his family. Small birds caught by tiny hands proved a tasty ingredient, too, as Albert Gillett recalls.

'Grandfather had a little straw stack for his pony and we would put a net over it in the late evening after all the sparrows had gone to roost. Then we'd go round with a sieve and rustle about in the straw and catch all the sparrows and, yes, break their necks, skin them, and cut their heads and feet off. Grandfather would make sparrow pies and we used to love them.'

Rural children certainly could not afford to be squeamish. From a young age they were often expected to be involved in some way in the killing of animals for food. It was all part of their training for farm work in later life. The most gruesome, dramatic ritual of all was the killing of the pig, usually taking place around autumn time, to provide fresh meat for the family during the winter months. Cyril Rice was brought up in Cwmbach, a village in mid-Wales in the 1920s.

'The pig was my job. Feed the pig in the morning and the evening, clean him out and look after him and you got quite friendly with him. Some funny thing to have as a pet, a pig, but you'd scratch his back and he'd love it and he'd be honk, honk and grunting fine. Then it would come to the time for the killing. The butcher would come; he slipped a leather thong over his head and drove him to a bench that was specially designed for the killing. The old pig, he put up a struggle then he gives that up. The butcher would get a knife and shave the hair from the neck where he's going to slit his throat. Now of course this was a bit like how I used to scratch him and old pig is honking again, he's quite enjoying it.

'Then the butcher would part the fat in the neck, then a turn of the knife. That cuts the jugular vein. The amount of blood that spurted out was terrible. Now, it was my job sometimes when I got a bit older to help hold the old pig down. I had to do it, but I was furious and sad. I used to swear I would never

Pig Killing Day at Crookhall, Durham. Feeding the family pig was usually the children's job.

touch a bit of it. The pig was hung up in the back kitchen, then he'd be jointed. But it was the smell of the cooking, the liver and faggots and spare ribs that always changed my mind. Nobody in this wide world could make liver and faggots like my mother. Oh, they were delicious.'

Fresh food and fresh air undoubtedly contributed to the fact that country children were generally healthier than those in the cities. But the contrast was nowhere near as great as has been assumed. Inadequate diet in large impoverished families, crumbling and overcrowded cottage homes, lack of sanitation and the slow development of health care and hospitals in the countryside all played their part in the high level of disease and death among village children in the first decades of the twentieth century. In the 1900s at least one baby in every ten born in country districts died before it reached its first birthday. In some counties such as Wiltshire, Herefordshire and Dorset a quarter of all recorded deaths were of children aged five or less. Epidemics of whooping cough, measles and tuberculosis, which had such a devastating effect in the cities, also took a heavy toll in the countryside.

When a child became ill, the poverty of the parents often prevented them from getting proper treatment from the doctor as they could not afford the bills. Parents often had little choice but to resort to traditional cures. Many people recall how raw onion or onion gruel (thin porridge) were used for, and often helped, sore throats and colds. But the folk remedies for more serious and life-threatening illnesses were often extremely dubious and far less successful. In East Anglia a common remedy for whooping cough until the 1930s was to feed the sick child with a fried mouse. In Oxfordshire they might be taken out to smell the sheep before breakfast. Some turned to herbalists, 'quack' doctors or gypsies for advice. Con Gray grew up in the village of Walters Ash in Buckinghamshire, and in 1917 her five-year-old sister Olive was diagnosed with tuberculosis.

'You couldn't afford proper medical treatment then and anyway, they didn't understand it. A gypsy woman said to my mother it could be cured if we put snails in a muslin bag and rubbed it anti-clockwise around her stomach. That was well known as a supposed cure for T.B. It was my job to collect all the snails, which I did. There were loads around the front of our cottage. My mother did this with the snails religiously like the gypsy said and Olive seemed to improve a bit. But I'm afraid she died after just a few months. I remember her little white coffin being carried away. After that my mum was always singing hymns in the home to cheer herself up.'

The family life of the country child was ruled less by physical punishment than in the cities. While the stern, moralistic approach of 'spare the rod, spoil the child' remained strong in urban areas before the last war, in the countryside corporal punishment for children was not so deeply entrenched. Many children brought up in villages in the south and east of England remember that their parents would rarely, if ever, smack or beat them. In the Shetlands, where evangelism had little influence, a unique, libertarian approach to child-rearing flourished. Here, among crofter families, corporal punishment was practically unheard of and parents controlled their children by reasoning with them. Children could talk during meals and could leave the table when they wished – freedoms rare among city children from all social classes at this time. Opposition to corporal punishment was so strongly felt by some rural parents that they would fiercely oppose teachers who caned their children at

Con Gray (bottom right) with her baby sister Olive (middle, right) who died from T.B. in 1917.

Children attend a lesson in Trimdon, Durham. Before the Second World War many rural teachers were untrained.

school. Arthur Burley attended Perranwell village school in Cornwall in the 1910s and vividly remembers his father's response after he had been so badly beaten by the school teacher that he had weal marks on his back.

'We went up to the master's house. Father said to him, "While I've been waiting for you to come out, I've noticed in your passage you've got a hall stand with walking sticks and umbrellas in there. Now, I could break all those walking sticks and umbrellas around your back but I aren't going to. But outside your gate is the King's highway and when you go out there – it may not be tomorrow mornin', it might not be the mornin' after, it might not even be this week – but one mornin' when you go out and you get down to the village I shall be waitin' for you with a stick." And he said, "I'm going to beat you with a stick right up through the village and the women in the village will see me doing it."'

The threat was never carried out, but as a result of it the schoolteacher's wife bought Arthur a new suit and he was never punished again.

Since the introduction of compulsory schooling in late-Victorian times, the standard of educational attainment in village schools remained low. Many smaller schools were housed in dilapidated buildings with few resources and just one or two teachers who struggled to teach the entire age range from five to fourteen. In 1936 about two-thirds of rural children were still educated in all-age schools. Most of the teachers were untrained – only a third of the teachers in rural schools had a teacher's certificate.

Elementary education in villages was often very basic, consisting of little more than rote learning of the 'Three Rs' and canings for those who stepped out of line. This kind of schooling had little appeal for children used to freedom and independence in the countryside. Those who lived on farms or in remote hamlets had to walk several miles to the village school every day. It could be such a long journey that some rode in. Reg Dobson, a farmer's son born in 1913, went to school in a Shropshire village.

'I used to go to school on a pony but he was a little beggar, and this one morning I was late for school and I was putting the bridle on and I'd fed him with some oats. 'Course he was chewing away and I put me finger in his mouth and he bit straight through it. So I was off school for a fortnight – that suited me all right. I was a farm boy and I wanted all me freedom. I'd been running wild and I didn't want the restrictions of school. I was always getting into trouble; I used to have the cane regular.'

Expectations were low and teachers often had trouble in controlling the children. Local custom and practice sometimes took precedence over the school rules. Betty Bailey grew up on an apple-growing farm in Herefordshire where, as a young child, she was a regular cider drinker.

'I started drinking cider when I was, oh, four or five years of age. I always had a barrel of my own, four gallons, with my name over the top and a small mug hung up on a nail above. Cider was always there; I was brought up with it, that was my drink, I thought everybody drank cider. I always drank cider for my lunch at school but I just had one catastrophe with it. We had a little desk then and as I pulled the top of the desk up, the cork flew out and it went up to the ceiling with a big pop. 'Course everybody started laughing. We had to mop it all up. But that

A schoolboy takes a break from blackberry picking. Many country children collected 'food for free' for the family table.

evening the vicar went down to see my mum and said, "I'm very sorry but she won't be able to bring any cider to school again.""

Work, not school, dominated the lives of most village children. The countryside, despite its sentimental associations with a free and 'natural' childhood was, in fact, the last bastion of child labour. School work sometimes took second place to work in the fields.

Right up to the Second World War the village school still bowed to seasonal agricultural demands. Farmers wanted cheap labour at busy times of the year and parents were keen for their children to earn extra money when necessities such as a child's annual pair of boots bit deeply into the family budget.

Harvest time usually fell in August during the school holiday, when children helped out as a matter of course. Not for nothing was it known as the Harvest Holiday. But if for any reason harvest was delayed or spilled over into a new school term, the older boys or girls would be missing. Every pair of hands was welcome in the fields. The children of small farmers with little cash to pay for seasonal labour would often be expected to miss school, if necessary, to work alongside their parents. Farmers wanted cheap labour at other busy times of the agricultural year, too, such as pea picking, fruit picking and hop picking.

In some counties such as rural Kent and Herefordshire, special holidays were arranged for children to get involved in the work. Otherwise children simply stayed away. With such hostile attitudes towards education there was a reluctance among local magistrates in many rural areas to prosecute parents for breaking school attendance regulations. Instead the village school adapted to the needs of the local economy.

The biggest exodus of village children out of the classroom and on to the land was during the First World War, when thousands of children were officially allowed to work to help the war effort. In Huntingdonshire, as early as July 1915, it was reported that around half of the county's boys between the ages of twelve and fourteen had been granted exemptions.

During the 1920s and 1930s actual truancy rates in areas such as rural Cambridgeshire and Essex remained as high as 20 per cent during peak times in the fields. Many school attendance officers patrolling the villages by foot or by bike were fighting a losing battle. George Cook grew up near Harlow Common in Essex during the 1920s. With his father unemployed for long periods the family were on parish relief and heavily dependent on young George's earnings in the fields.

'We were kept home from school to go pea picking when they were in season, possibly towards the end of June onwards. You'd be picking peas from about five o'clock in the morning until about three in the afternoon. And suddenly the cry

would go up, "Look out the school board man's here!" Someone would always be watching. And I've never seen such a scramble. The pea bine [a long climbing stem] would be in heaps all over the field and you'd just do a vanishing trick and hide under these pea bines until the school board man, Mr. Salmon, had gone. If he'd only pulled one of these heaps of pea bines to one side he'd have found kids underneath, but he never did.'

Most young boys like these pictured stacking hay at Aberdyfan, Dyfed, ended up working on farms after leaving school.

In the mid-1920s it was estimated only about 5 per cent of entrants to secondary schools in rural areas were the children of agricultural labourers, then the predominant occupation. Men and women now in their eighties and nineties tell a familiar story of passing their exams for the grammar school but having their hopes for a bright future quickly squashed as parents couldn't afford the uniform and other school requirements. The lengthy and difficult journey to the school from their remote country home proved another real stumbling block. In the 1900s children usually left school on their twelfth birthday; in the 1910s the official age was thirteen; and in the 1920s, with the extension of the compulsory school-leaving age, pupils would normally leave on their fourteenth birthday. As soon as they could leave school, rural children were immediately looking for full-time work. Dutiful sons and daughters who had watched their well-loved parents struggle to make ends meet were both obliged and often proud to do it. Parents expected nothing less.

Many boys and girls were traditionally employed at centuries-old hiring or mop fairs, which survived up to the 1920s and 1930s, especially in rural Scotland, in the agricultural north of England and in parts of Northern Ireland and Wales. In market towns such as Ulverston in the Lake District they usually took place twice a year – at Whitsuntide in May and at Martinmas in November. Youngsters would line up in the market-place to be inspected and questioned by farmers, many of whom were local. Some, however, travelled from other districts to recruit boys and girls. Would-be workers might carry a bundle of clothing with them to show they were available for hire.

If the children were considered suitable, a fee for a six-month or one-year contract would be agreed. Once the children had accepted the farmer's 'penny' – in reality usually a shilling (5p) – they were bound to the farmer. For many, living away from home for the first time, it would be a harsh and brutal initiation into the adult world.

Country children and adults often found work at hiring fairs like this one in Burford, Oxfordshire at the turn of the century. In some rural areas the fairs survived up to the 1920s and 1930s.

Iden Times, Burford Hiring Fair.   № 52.

Joe Risby

Joe Risby was born in 1911 and grew up in the Suffolk village of Lavenham. He was the son of a farm labourer who won the Distinguished Conduct Medal in the Boer War.

Oh, I loved the head of the rabbit at dinner. I broke it up so I could suck the pale, white brains out. Then I ate all the rabbit off the skull. We lived on rabbits: rabbit pie, rabbit soup, rabbit dumplings; every part of the rabbit was used. Beautiful food. My dad used to snare 'em on the farm where he worked. He'd put down about half a dozen snares the previous night and when he went to work in the morning he might have a couple of rabbits and he'd put 'em in a ditch and cover 'em in grass – 'cos that was a crime, catching rabbits – and at night he put them in a bag to bring home.

You was a hungry boy back then, hungry all the time. They were really hard times but I did enjoy 'em. We used to play lovely games like rounders and spin tops. You'd go up and down the street with the spin top and the whip, and keep on twisting it round from one end of the street to the other – there was no motors in Lavenham. Fred Huffy, the blacksmith, would make us a hoop about three feet in diameter and you'd go round the village with this hoop and an iron rod so you could control it.

We used to have eating competitions, too, in the harness maker's shop. We'd have about six bananas, all peeled, laid out on clean paper in front of us. Ben, the referee, used to bang the table with a hammer to start the contest. You'd pick up a banana with the left hand and the one who showed the cleanest mouth at the end of six bananas was the winner. One day things went wrong when we had an ice-cream contest with cornets all laid out. Ikey Simpson, that was his nickname, suddenly his face went blue and down he went on the floor. The ice cold had hit his stomach.

Farm children in Fife proudly display their catch. Rabbits were a crucial – and popular – part of the countryman's diet.

The days went too quick, then, no doubt about it. I loved the village. When you was a little boy you never passed a woman or a man without speaking to 'em: 'Good morning Mrs Brown.' 'Good morning, boy.' You always addressed any man as a 'boy' here. In fact you could say he was a boy from nine to ninety! A lot of us had nicknames. My grandfather was called 'Slave', my father was called 'Slave' and they called me 'Young

Slave'. I always worked hard, you see. I think the population in Lavenham was 1800 and you knew practically all of them. You would know if someone was ill and, say, a week later you heard the church bell tolling for five minutes you knew so-and-so had died.

My own brother George died at twenty-four – he drowned in the River Stour. Fred Jarvis, who worked for the undertaker, brought him home in a lorry covered with tarpaulin. I helped carry the coffin up the steps and put me poor brother down. In that day and age the coffin remained in the room until they were buried. Fred said to me, 'Joe, can I use your privy?'

I said, 'Yes, Fred.'

'Do you want to see your brother?'

'Yes.'

He took the lid off and went down the privy. I looked at my brother and thought to myself, 'No, he is asleep, he must be asleep.' He looked lovely, me brother did, as though he was in a deep sleep. I touched his face and it was deathly cold. And when Fred came back I had a good mind to tell him he was asleep but, no, I knew he couldn't lay there so quiet.

On the day of the funeral the pall-bearers came to the cottage. The custom then was to give each a bottle of beer before they left. When they'd drunk it, Mr Deacon, the man in charge in a big top hat, said, 'Does anybody want a last look?' Then they screwed the lid down and carried him down the steps on to the bier. The pall-bearers and Mr Deacon marched in front to Lavenham church. All the people in the street pulled down their blinds in respect for the person who'd gone. As soon as the cortège was done, the blinds would go up again.

I missed my brother George terribly. It was him who got me into trouble once at school. Sometimes, if you couldn't spell a word, you'd get your ear clipped as much as to say, 'Wake up!' When I told George he said, 'You know what you want to do. When they ask you to read again and you come to a word you can't read, you say "cartwheel".'

I was only a little boy and I thought, He must know, he's eight years older than me.' So when the teacher said to me, 'Risby, stand up and read from page three' and I came to this word I couldn't understand, I said, "cartwheel". The teacher looked at me strangely but didn't say anything. I came to another word. "Cartwheel".

She came along and said, 'Where's this word "cartwheel", Risby?'

I said, 'My brother told me.'

'Brother?!'

She gave me a real smash on my ear. My brother did laugh when I told him. They smacked you for the slightest thing, but it was good for ye. Wonderful discipline. I loved every minute of school.

After school and on Saturdays I used to do jobs. I used to look forward to being with my relation, a farm worker, whose nickname was Gunner Barrel. He says to me,

'Joe, you can help me with the Brussels sprouts. They've got to go to Covent Garden.' So I used to go there after school in the dark, picking sprouts. And me poor old hands would be cold. He used to rub my hands. I loved it when he done that. He rubbed me hands and tied a sack around my waist because they used to be wet from the stalks. I thought the world of me Gunner Barrel, especially when he rubbed me hands. That was love, that was.

When I left school I'd have loved to have been an engine driver. I used to watch the trains and run on the bridge just outside the station to see them come underneath. I wanted to drive one day and see the corn growing higher every day and see everything changing in the countryside as the days went by. If my father had been an engine driver there was a very good chance I would have been, but he was a farm worker and I finished up on the farm the same.

A young boy learns to plough the traditional way in Kingsdown, Kent in 1936 – at a time when horsepower ruled.

I got my first job at the age of fourteen. I'd been wandering the streets of Lavenham for about a fortnight. It was crowded with unemployed men. Jobs were gold dust. I met a farmer I knew and he says to me in his booming voice, 'Hello bor', what you doing on?'

'I finished school.'

'Ain't you got no work?'

'No Mr Dewar.'

'Go up to the farm, they will give you a job.'

My first pay packet was ten bob. I had a four-mile walk from work. I couldn't get home quick enough. It took me an hour. I couldn't wait to give some money to my mum to help pay the rent. I was proud to help the household; not just me, my brothers and sisters, too. What do you call it – dedication?

Marjorie Riddaway

Born in 1907, Marjorie Riddaway grew up on a small farm near the village of Atherington in North Devon. The ninth of ten children, her daily tasks included feeding the pigs, delivering milk and collecting hen's eggs. Her mother was beset with serious ill health throughout Marjorie's childhood and died when Marjorie was just fourteen. Marjorie married a farmer and had two sons and two daughters.

Marjorie Riddaway (aged six). Like many farmers' daughters of the time, she was taken out of school to work.

I did miss quite a lot of schooling. During the First World War we used to pick basketfuls and basketfuls of moss in school time about a mile and a half from the village because there was a shortage of cotton wool at the time and this certain moss was very absorbent. And I used to help my mum a lot because sometimes she would get an order and we'd have to stay at home and pick a bit more fruit.

But I didn't have to be encouraged to stay at home because I didn't get on with the teacher. I used to get a hiding off her for spelling mistakes and bad writing. You were hit for everything, especially if you weren't teacher's pet. You had to hold out your hand and have so many stripes of the stick if you were displeasing her. Sometimes you wondered what for. Everything depended on the mood of that teacher. I used to get so sick of being punished and tired of trying so, no, I wasn't a bit worried about missing school.

I thoroughly enjoyed helping Mum. Like the majority of farmers' wives she always went to market to run her stall. In the summer she used to go to Bideford market on Tuesday, Barnstaple market on Friday, and on Saturday she would go to Torrington market with all the fruit. Fruit was a very, very valuable thing in north Devon. We grew a lot on the farm we lived on. We children used to pick lots of black-currants and raspberries. Boy, you'd get tired when you were just a child of about ten.

Your fingers would really ache and you'd get fed up. But we had to do it and we did it. I'd put punnets and punnets full of raspberries in a big maun [wicker or woven basket with handles] ready for market.

It was a real outing to go with Mother. You had quite a bit of space to spread out the butter and cream Mother made, and the fruit and vegetables like swedes, potatoes and parsnips which Father tilled in the garden. If we'd killed a pig, Mother sold the pudding she made from the intestines and various bits of the pig. Mother, like the other women, wore a nice white starched apron with pockets, coppers on one side and silver on the other. If she was busy with two or three people at a time it would be like a shop. I would serve the customers just like Mum would because I was very good at sums.

She used to sell dozens of flowers for ha'penny and a penny a pound. I was usually on the flowers side of the stall and Mother was on the other, weighing the cream. I used to pick all sorts of flowers from the hedges for Mother: pussy willow, violets, snowdrops and primroses and I picked nice big leaves and rested the flowers on them so that the stall used to look lovely and decorative. If I was collecting bunches of daffodils and snowdrops I used to reckon it up in my mind and think, 'Mum will soon have enough to buy me a new coat.'

Life is an adventure isn't it when you're young? I was always thinking about tomorrow and thinking, 'I wonder what will happen. Will the cow calf or will we catch any more rabbits to go to market?' I was always waiting for tomorrow.

Marian Atkinson

Born in 1905, Marian Atkinson grew up in a small, isolated community in the Lake District. She was one of seven girls and her father was the captain of the passenger steamers on the Lakes. She was taught how to skin a rabbit, pluck a chicken, bake bread and starch and iron a shirt until it was stiff as cardboard.

All the children at Railway Cottages loved the wood. It was right opposite, over the cart road where the baker's and butcher's vans used to come down and over a small field. We were always given instructions: 'Now if you're going up in the wood today, fetch a bundle of wood home for the fire or bring a log.' We got our faggots, tied 'em up with a piece of string, put them by the wall and then played. We older ones always had to look after the younger children. We used to put the little ones down on moss or leaves and then go picking crab apples or wild damsons, sloes or blackberries. We always took a bucket so we could take some home. I loved climbing the trees. I was the tomboy of the family and knew how to look after myself. I once knocked out one of Sidney Lamb's front teeth with a stick because he tried to pull me out of a tree.

I loved fighting. For our row of twelve cottages there was an old-fashioned pump for clean drinking water and there was a trough to catch the water. Mother told me one day to fetch some water so I went with two buckets. When I got there Elsie Webb came along with her buckets and said, 'I was here first.' I said, 'No you weren't, I was here first so get out of the way.' She pushed me so I pushed her into the trough. I had her down on her hands and knees and I just lifted the handle and had a couple of good pumps and wet her through. She scrambled out of the trough and ran home screaming her head off. Mrs Webb came knocking at the front door with her by the hand, wringing wet through. 'Look what your Marion has done to our Elsie.' Of course, I had to admit that I had done it. We never told lies.

All us children used to walk about two and a half miles to school each day. We accumulated at the big gate and when we got over the river bridge we met the boy and girl from the smithy and Lesley and Mildred Wren from the post office and Freddie Dickinson from the orchard, and we all walked to school. But instead of going all the way round the road we used to dive over a hedge and across the farmer's field because it used to cut half a mile off the journey. We'd see the turnips, potatoes or cabbage and decide what we'd pinch on the way home. On the way back the bigger boys used to say, 'Keep your eye rolling for the farmer.' My parents wouldn't accept anything stolen – they used to make us take it back – so we used to sit under a hedge and gnaw the vegetables like a rabbit. At that time there was no tractors. It was all horses and carts.

Children receiving a village education. In the mid-1920s it was estimated only 5 per cent of entrants to secondary school were the children of farm labourers.

A Scottish farm servant. For many servants being able to milk a cow was a condition of employment.

If we could hear the farmers' horses clop-clopping, we used to bung what we'd been eating under the hedge and go like lightning back home, large as life.

The village school was small with about forty pupils and two teachers: Mr Taylor and Miss Dixon. There was a partition between the two classrooms and every morning when we had religious service that partition was pulled back and we all stood. We sang a hymn and then Mr Taylor read this little bit out of the Bible. He would tell us all about the war and what the Kaiser was doing. And then he'd say, 'I have the sad news to tell you children that Mrs Dickinson's boy Ted – or whoever it was – has been killed in the trenches.' We would all say a prayer and Mr Taylor would get a whole sheet of foolscap and we all signed the names on this to say how very sorry we were and it went to the boy's family.

At eleven I passed the exam to go to the grammar school but my parents weren't in a position to clothe me or buy the books so it never came to nothing. I started work at fourteen on a farm as a servant. The food was good but I was a dogsbody and worked long hours from six o'clock in the morning 'til about eight o'clock at night. It was general farm work: washing buckets and picking stones in the green pastures so the mowing machines didn't hit them and blunt the blades.

The farmer gave me some tripe one day to clean. Now when the tripe comes out of a cow it's green. You pump water on it and you get a knife and scrape the green off 'til it becomes white but you have to pump it dozens of times. I did it to the best of my ability and as I was coming out of the dairy he said, 'Let's have a look at the tripe. . . Call that done!' And with his clog he tried to kick me bottom but he got me in the back of the knees and down I went on the floor. The missus came out and consoled me and said he didn't mean it. He was a bit of a drinker. But I sulked and cried and said, 'I'm not stopping here.'

So that night when I went to bed, I put three petticoats, three pairs of knickers and three frocks on so I didn't need to carry them. I put all me odds and ends in a canvas bag. I waited until they were in bed and crept out. It was an eight-mile journey home. I went across the fields and climbed over the stone walls and sat on the gates and had a good cry. I was terrified to death, imagining all sorts of things like bulls running loose in the fields and attacking me. Eventually I got home before dinner the next day. Mother saw me through the kitchen window. 'What the devil are you doing 'ere?' I said, 'I've run away. He kicked me.' Of course she cuddled me and loved me and said, 'You're not going back there.' About two years later I met up with his daughter at the hiring fair and she told me that I wasn't the only one that had run away. There was seven boxes in the barn where the girls had run away and left them.

I was still only fourteen when I started going to the hiring fairs at Ulverston which were at Whitsuntide and Martinmas, which was in November. You used to stand on one side of the street. The farmers stood on the other side by the County Hotel. They would walk up and down and look you up and down. One would say, 'Are you for hire?'

'Yes'.

Children from Muggleswick, Durham in 1917. It was a Victorian tradition for young people to dress up in the uniform of the job they were seeking.

'*What can you do? Can you milk?*' *If you could milk you said so.*
'*Can you bake?*'

They had a whole list of things. They'd say, 'What are you asking?' I always remember my first hiring when I asked for £15 for six months. He said, 'What! £15. I'll be bankrupt. I'll give you £10.' In the end he beat me down to £12. 10s. He'd say, 'Right lass' and he would lift his hand up, spit on it and then pat his hand against mine. Then I got the shilling and was hired. I couldn't back out then. Even if another fellow came along and offered me £15.

We always looked forward to the hiring fairs. We were free, off the rein of the boss or mistress, or mother or father. We all went in gangs because a lot of us had gone to school together. The hiring was usually over by one o clock. We'd go to the fish shop and have a packet of chips in newspaper with salt and vinegar, and ice cream, which we never had at home. Then off we tore down to where the fairground was. There was swing boats, hobby horses, stalls where you could buy ribbons, buttons and knick-knacks. Everything you could want.

Of course we canoodled with the lads and had a sneaky kiss. This one boy said he would take me on the swing boats. He got in the boat and this girl jumped in the swing boat in front of me.

I said, 'I'm going with that lad.'

She said, 'I was here first.'

I said, 'Well you're last now,' and pulled her out and dumped her on the floor. Oh, she squared up to me and clouted me but I clouted her back and won. I got on the swing boat and had me swing.

Gordon Anderson

Gordon Anderson grew up in Newmains in Central Scotland with his three brothers and sister and his disabled father who worked on the railways. He left home in 1934, when he was thirteen, to work as a farm hand. But his experience on a farm in the Borders disillusioned him. When he was eighteen, shortly before the outbreak of the Second World War, he volunteered for the army.

My mother wanted me out of bed sharp that morning. 'I'm taking you to Lanark market', she said.

I said, 'What for?'

'For a job on the farm.'

I still wasn't fourteen. It was a sunny day in June and we took a bus to the cattle market. My mother asked one of the people where the farmers went when they were

A shy Gordon Anderson, pictured while still a schoolboy.

looking for people to work and we made our way there. I was just kicking about, watching the scene, when I heard this old farmer say to my mother, 'Is he for feeing?'

My mother says 'Yes'.

He says, 'He's awfully wee'.

Mother said, 'Aye, but he's willing and he can milk'.

He said, 'Aye, but he's awfully wee. . . I'll try him at £11 a year.' He took a piece of paper out of his pocket which Mother signed and he gave her 2s, the signing-on fee.

My mother didn't say goodbye. She just said, 'I'm away to get my bus. You just wait there.' All I had was my brown paper parcel with an extra pair of boots and my father's knitted socks in it. I hung about listening to the auctioneers calling out until, eventually, I got a lift to the farm with a cattle float driver, which the farmer had arranged. It was sitting among the cattle that I started to think I might not see my brothers and my sister for a time and I cried. But it was a bit of an adventure, too. I thought, 'I must be grown up to be earning £11,' and I wanted to help my mother as she had five of us.

When we arrived at the farm the driver said to me, 'I'm sorry for you son, coming to a place like this. Come on, I'll show you where the bothie [accommodation] is. I would na' put an animal in it.' He opened the door of this place. It was small. The fireplace had been bricked up. There were old blankets on the bed so I went and turned them over. 'What are you looking for?' he asked.

'Sheets', I said.

'There are none,' he said. The pillow was a big, long, bolster-type thing full of chaff so the thistles would come through and stick into you.

The work was so hard and tedious; the same thing day after day. I was shy and small for my age, not much more than four feet ten. I'd have to milk the cows and deliver the milk to the houses before breakfast. The churns nearly broke my back: they were nearly as big as me. After, I'd have to fill up and wheel out about seven barrows of muck and I had to hose down the cattle's behinds, hose out the byre [cow shed] and brush it out. That was really hard work. There were three horses and I had to groom them and clean their stables. I worked from five o'clock in the morning until it was dark. Seven days a week. I never had one day off.

I took the 'flu once and collapsed by lunch-time. The next thing I knew I came round in the bothie. The boy-friend of Jeannie, the farmer's daughter, had carried me in. 'He'll not be fit to work,' he said. 'Aye, he will. My dad says he's got to be up at work at five o'clock,' she said. I was going about like a rag doll, I didn't know whether I was walking or thinking straight. The farmer kept saying 'You'll work it off.'

Many were the times I was so exhausted I'd drag one leg after another, incapable of thinking. When the farmer asked me to do some harrowing I told him I wasn't fit to do it but he was going to hit me with his stick, so I just hooked the horses to the harrow and walked up and down with them like someone who was there but wasn't there. It's a hard thing when you're fourteen years of age to face up to a man of about fifty-five because he'd always try to beat you with the crook he carried if you told him you were overworked.

I was hungry most of the time because the food was unreal. Mainly pieces of meat, dreadful looking, floating on the top of pure grease. Sometimes you had a slice of bread. They made butter on the farm but, oh no, you weren't allowed butter on your bread. I used to go and eat as much as I could of the cattle food, large brown beans, because they were sweet.

It was six months before my mother came to collect my pay: £5 10s. Oh, aye, I told her I hated it. I told her about the food. 'You'll get used to it, son,' she said. 'That's farm life.' So I sort of made up my mind I'd have to stick it out for the next six months.

Well, by this time it was really into winter, a bad winter, and the bothie was the coldest place. When the farmer banged on the door at five o'clock I'd try and look for my boots in the pitch black. They'd be absolutely frozen to the floor because they were soaking wet

Weary-looking boys stook corn at Weare Giffard, Devon in the early 1900s.

when I'd taken them off. Then I'd kick them to get them broken and put them on. It was like putting your feet into an ice pool. When I went into the byre I was glad to start milking just to get some heat through me. At first it was very painful because your hands were so frozen. You'd have to knock the ice off the top of the pail of water, put your hand and dirty cloth into the freezing water, put a bit of black soap on the cloth and clean the cows' udders. The pain would come into your hands as they got warm.

You never slept much even though you were very tired because the cold kept you awake most of the time. I used to wait until the family was all in bed. When I saw the lights going out I used to creep into the byre and get an armful of straw and put it down beside two of the quiet cows lying down. I'd sleep with them to get the heat from them. The only thing was I couldn't hear the farmer knocking me up and he kicked up an awful row once he found out where I was sleeping.

When it turned to spring I started to realize what had really happened to me. I was no longer a person: I was a thing. I knew I stunk to the high heavens. I wasn't allowed a bath. I thought to myself, 'Even the rabbits coming out of these burrows don't smell the way I do.' What could be worse than feeling that you are worse than an animal? An animal went out in the rain and got washed with the rain whereas I got soaked often and as soon as the wind dried my clothes on me the smell was still there.

When the year was up my mother came to get the rest of my pay. I was out cutting thistles in the field. When I came in I was so pleased to be going home. My mother said, 'I've fee'd you on for another year, son. I'm sorry but we cannae take you – we haven't room at home.' I broke down and screamed. I said, 'You cannot do that!'

I went to the bothie, packed up my bits and pieces in the same brown paper I'd had when I arrived and just started to run blindly through the rain. It was coming down in buckets. The police picked me up three hours later. I had run for twenty miles, nearly. I was exhausted with crying, exhausted with running. The police explained that my mother had signed me on for another year and as I was still a minor she and the farmer could hold me to it.

I never felt hatred for anyone in my life the way I felt hatred for my mother. I had to go back and stay the whole year and life got harder. [When he was sixteen, Gordon finally left the farm and was reunited with his family.]

Albert Gillett

Albert Gillett, born in 1923 in the Cambridgeshire Fens, has always loved reading, partly to make up for the time when he was systematically removed from school to do farm work. In the post-war years Albert took over his father's coal merchant business in the former village of Black Horse Drove where he grew up.

Country children
were expected to
help in the fields
after school and
at weekends to
earn money.

I always felt that I was a slave. Because my father worked on the farm and lived in a tied cottage I had to work hard for the farmer too. It was part of the system being carried on all over the Fens. It wasn't written down but if a man worked on a farm the eldest son, at least, had to work on that farm to keep the father's job and the accommodation secure.

I'd work on Saturdays, evenings, doing all the menial tasks on a farm at a very early age, much earlier than most other boys had to. Even as a small boy of five years old I would have to go out in the fields at certain seasons. I remember my father would be digging potatoes with a fork, my mother would be picking them up and I would be behind with a big basket – as big as myself – picking up what we called 'the chats', which were small potatoes for the pigs.

I often used to work after school at four o'clock. I had to do everything Father told me. Often I would have to take the bullocks out down the farm to graze on the grass down the side of the road and stop them from going in the crops, or take them out on the riverbank to feed. I would have to fill great big bags of chaff to put in the mangers to feed the horses and bullocks. Or I'd grind mangels [beet] for them and mix meal, water and boiled potatoes for the pigs. In the winter I'd help with jobs like sugar beet. It would be very cold and wet, and I would have to go out in the field with a fork and put the beet into little heaps in the field so that the workers could come along and throw them in the carts. When I was a bit older I'd have to handle these beets, knock them clean, lay them level and chop them off with a chopper. Anything to keep me hard at work. Although I was small I was pretty tough and will power, I suppose, got me through. But I always felt I was being used and I was always trying to get away from it.

Albert Gillett (far left) with his beloved violin. He was unable to pursue his education full-time and was made to work in the fields instead.

I made up for it at school. Without boasting, I was near the top of the class and right through my schooling I didn't excel but I did good. Always I had books at home I'd either borrowed or had from the library. I read them through and through and through until I lived them. I would sit reading beside a candle or under the covers of my bed by torch. When we were asked at school if we would like to learn to play the violin, I seized the opportunity. I had to ask Dad for a penny a week for my violin lessons. I shall never understand it but he said, 'Yes'. A penny a week was a lot of money in those days for my parents because they had six children. I always wanted to learn things. I had the urge to do, to get on, not be kept down by the agricultural system operating in the 1930s.

Education was not important in the Fens. If your father worked on the farm you knew where you were going. You were going on the farm. As I was tied to my father's job I was taken from school for farm work during the seasonal times of year. Over the last three years I did miss quite a bit of my education. At thirteen and a half years of age I never went back to school again.

I won't say I was miserable but I always desired something better. I felt I deserved it. On some of the evenings I had to myself I used to go round to another farm because the farmer had bought a new three-wheel John Deere tractor, a little one. Well, it's like a boy today looking at a jet aircraft and saying, 'I'm going to fly that.' I wanted to drive this tractor and this farmer let me drive it in the evenings, under supervision. I wasn't very old, about fourteen, but it was my pride and joy. This farmer said I could come and work for him driving the tractor. Well, that was all I was looking for. I felt it was a step up. So when I got home I said to Father, 'Dad, I've got a job.'

Dad said, 'Yes, I know you have, you work here.'

I said, 'No, I've got a job tractor driving.'

But he said no way. 'You work here because I work here.' And that was it.

My father lived for his work. He was a very hard worker and had worked for this same farmer for fourteen years, all my life, but it didn't last. I remember this day as plain as if it were now. We were in the bottom field of the farm, hoeing potatoes in June time. My father was in front of me about twenty yards away. The farmer walked past me and went up to my father. They talked and after a little time the farmer threw his hat up in the air and stamped on it. I heard him swearing at my dad and shouting, 'I've had the best fourteen years of your life! I'm finished with you!' His employment was terminated right then and we were to be evicted from our cottage.

Mother broke down in tears and sat crying and holding my oldest sister when she heard. She didn't know where we were going and what we'd do. One thing always stays in my mind. The cottages then were always dark and dingy with small windows and no electric light, and I can remember how oppressive and depressing it felt to me. With this happening it was like the black hole of Calcutta. I felt the farmer wanted shooting after all my father – and me – had done for him. I hoped he'd go bankrupt and have nothing left. It turned me more against the farming attitude because this was the thing on farms. The farmer, for the least little thing and without provocation, he'd sack a man if he thought he would. There was no protection, you see.

Against all the odds Dad found a derelict cottage available from a farmer, but there was no room for all we children so we were farmed out. I remember quite plainly I went to sleep at my grandmother's. It was about two years before the new council houses were built and father put his name down and got a new council house with three bedrooms. Then he became a free agent and could work where he liked.

In a way, I was glad we got evicted. It showed me a glint of light, an escape from the tyranny of what had been taking place. When the war came along I volunteered for the Air Force at seventeen. Now I've got to be truthful, I didn't volunteer for entirely patriotic reasons. I did it to get away from the hard graft and the cold, wet, dirty conditions of farming. But, of course, I had to wait until I was eighteen before I was called up. After having been through what I'd been through on a farm, I found the RAF a real cushy life. Warmth, good clothing, companionship. It was real heaven, to me.

Ed Mitchell

The son of the village shoe and boot repairer, Ed Mitchell was born in 1916 and grew up in Chedgrave and later in Loddon in south Norfolk. After serving with the Grenadier Guards during the Second World War, Ed returned to Norfolk and worked at Midland Bank as a messenger until his retirement.

Valentine's Day was a very special day for us boys and girls in the village. There was this custom I've never knowed happen anywhere else. We'd congregate down the bottom of our road at about half past six in the morning and start at the big houses, like the rectory, where the posh people lived and sing this song.

> *Old Mother Valentine!*
> *Draw up your window blind,*
> *You be the giver,*
> *I'll be the taker.*

We'd chant this song over and over, quicker and quicker. The posh people would heat up ha'pennies and a few pennies on a shovel over a coal fire and throw 'em out of the window to us, red hot. Us children would scramble on the gravel and pick them up and bloody hell

Ed Mitchell (first row, far right) at school in the Norfolk village of Chedgrave.

they burnt. So you'd drop 'em right quick, I can tell you. If you put 'em in your trouser pocket they'd burn a hole in it. The big pots would be at their top window laughing their heads off. Then we'd move off down the street singing the Old Mother Valentine song. We'd speed it up and speed it up; you could hear us chanting all over the village.

At the grocer's, out would come the shopkeeper, old Harbourne. He'd throw rotten oranges and apples what had been left over from Christmas out in the road, and a few sweets if you were lucky. It was about quarter to seven in the morning, a bit dark you see, so from the lights of the shop we'd see what was on the road, pick it up and stuff it in our pockets. It was a kind of begging, that's what it was. We'd stop at other places and keep going until we came to the village of Loddon. We'd stop there because you'd get the Loddonite kids coming the other way singing the song and we'd have a bit of a fight, trying to get oranges off one another.

Kids used to play by the seasons in them days. The countryside was our playground, really. In March, boys would go bird-nesting. 'Course, every boy out in the country had a collection of birds' eggs in a box with glass over the top of it. There were plenty of birds about in them days: thrushes, blackbirds, blue-tits, yellow-hammers. We'd only take one egg from each nest, though. We'd put the eggs under our peaked cap. If old Amos the gamekeeper caught you down Chedgrave Common or in his plantations, he'd shout, 'What you boys up to?' Then he'd smack us on top of our heads so all the egg-shell and yolk would run down our face. He'd whack your arse hard, too, with a stick for disturbing the pheasants and partridges. There were also hundreds of water-hens down on the marshes and to get the eggs we had a long pole with a tablespoon tied on the end and we'd reach out into the reeds and scoop up the egg. They were really tasty boiled.

Come May or June us boys would swim in the river Ched, up to our ankles in black, creamy mud. We all learnt to swim there. We got a bicycle tube, you see, and put it round our neck and round our shoulders and then round our back and swam with it. Boys often went in the river 'show cock' because we couldn't afford costumes. One of the jobs of P.C. Hall, the village slop, was to superintend the boys swimming in the river naked. Boys weren't allowed in naked at twelve or thirteen. He used to hide in the five-foot high nettles. He didn't mind the young boys up to twelve in the cold water 'cos he said it looked like a 'peeled prawn on a walnut'! But anybody over that age, when they started growing hair anywhere other than the top of the head, he'd have 'em. He'd grab you as you were climbing up the bank, ask yer name and age and you'd be up Loddon Town Hall and get fined five bob.

Everyone was really scared stiff of P.C. Hall, especially the kids. He had come out of the Coldstream Guards, you see, and he was an imposing figure. He lived in a little cottage in the street and he used to stand outside his gate with his cape over his shoulders and his big helmet on, watching you. One day I was going past him to go to school and he grabbed me round the neck and said, 'Come here, boy, I want a word with you!'

Pilfering vegetables from farmers' fields was a common crime practised by hungry children.

He took me down the garden path by the scruff of the neck, opened his garden shed door and pushed me in. Cor! He was a big bloke, about six foot two. He looked like a bloody mountain to me.

'Now then, boy,' he said, 'I want to know why you pulled those two rows of sugar beet up by the path you come down from church to school.'

I said I didn't do it but he said, 'Yes you did. I got a witness to say you done it. Saw you pull 'em up. Now why did you do it?'

I said, 'I didn't do it!' and I hadn't done it neither.

He said, 'Well, this'll do for now,' and he gave me such a smack it nearly knocked me over. I ran like hell off to school, my ear ringing and tears streaming down my face. When I told my dad later what happened he said, 'Well, a good clip round the lug from P.C. Hall never done anybody any harm.'

Mind you, sometimes I'd take a swede home from one of the fields, which I shouldn't have done. I'd run home and give it to Mum. Loads of us were doing it. You'd go up to the fields about four or five o'clock in the afternoon, burrow in and get one or two swedes out, put the muck back on again, hit it with your hand and smooth it down again. I was frightened of being caught but a couple of swedes would do three or four dinners and Mum needed the food to keep the family going.

That was the same with the rabbits we killed in the harvest fields. I used to climb up a big tree in the plantation and listen to the still summer day to see if I could hear a binder going for miles away. Then I'd run home and get my rabbiting stick and a bottle of lemonade and a sandwich and march off to the sound where the binder was coming from. All the corn in them days was cut by two horses pulling a binder. The binder would go round and round and round until they got to the middle where the rabbits were hiding in the standing corn. As the corn got smaller the rabbits bolted out. Us kids used to run after them with the sticks shouting, 'Ooh, ooh, go there! Look! Go there!' 'Course the rabbits got confused, darting all over the place. Some kids could run quicker than others and you'd go arse over head over the stubble and that stubble was sharp, I'll tell you, 'cos you never had long trousers on. If the rabbits got in the hedge they'd gone. Otherwise you'd knock 'em on the head with the stick.

All the rabbits were laid out on the binder canvas and the farmer used to dish them out. Others got their share first, like the cowman, the horseman and the farm labourers. Us boys used to watch with our eyes bulging, hoping, hoping he'd give us a rabbit. It fed the family for about a couple of days, a rabbit did. Many's the time we knocked three or four rabbits on the head but there weren't enough to go round and you didn't get one. I'd go home and say, 'I ain't got a rabbit today, Mum.' She'd say, 'Never mind, perhaps you'll get one tomorrow.'

At harvest-time boys killed rabbits bolting from their hiding-place in the corn.

– Two –

To the Manor Born

Charles Aldred, a defiant eleven-year-old schoolboy in the village of Sotterley in Suffolk, was summoned to a showdown with the parson at the rectory. His crime was that he had not touched his cap to the displeased squire. Although this episode would not be out of place on the pages of a Victorian novel, it happened in 1931.

'The parson gave me the option of punishment. I could either have a kick up the backside or I could put on the boxing gloves with him. He was a bit of a boxer. Well, I was a half-tidy boy with fighting so I took a chance, but he laid me out. "Let that be a lesson to you, boy," he said. "Next time you see the squire you

Eaton Hall, the Gothic family seat of the Duke of Westminster in Cheshire.

touch your cap to him." You didn't dare tell your parents because you'd get another clip when you went home.'

It was not uncommon early this century for children to be chastised, and even caned, for forgetting – or refusing – to touch their cap to the people from the 'Hall'. Girls and boys were trained from a young age by the parson, teachers and their parents to respect and accept the upper-class authority and ritual deference which went hand-in-hand. The semi-feudal order of the countryside was a long time dying. In fact many aspects of the traditional master and servant relationship survived up to the Second World War. It was based on the extraordinary wealth of the landed classes.

In the late Victorian era some three-quarters of Britain was owned by 7,000 people. One quarter of England and Wales alone was in the hands of just 710 citizens. Top landowners were the Duke of Sutherland, who owned 1.25 million acres, and the Duke of Buccleuch with some 460,000 acres. The New Domesday Survey of 1873 noted more than forty other estates with more than 100,000 acres, most of which remained intact until the early twentieth century.

The great estates bore some resemblance to little kingdoms, each with an aristocratic leader at its head. Their ownership of vast tracts of land gave them immense influence and proprietorial rights not only over agriculture on the estate, but also over its minerals, its game, its politics, its clergy and, most importantly, over the local population. The most aristocratic counties were Rutland and Northumberland, where around half the land surface comprised great estates. After this (in descending order) came Nottinghamshire, Dorset, Wiltshire, and lastly Cheshire, the family seat of the Duke of Westminster, where more than a third of all land was held by the aristocracy.

Beneath the aristocracy in the rural hierarchy came the landed gentry, defined in the New Domesday Survey as owners of estates of up to 10,000 acres, which was 3,000 strong. Then there was the squirarchy, made up of 2,000 or so squires with holdings of around 1,000 to 3,000 acres. In the 1900s, around nine-tenths of all farmland was owned by the rural upper classes.

The fortunes of the aristocracy and gentry began to decline, for some dramatically, immediately after the First World War as a result of death duties, high taxation and the agricultural depression that saw rents from their farms fall. They were forced to sell off parts, or all, of their estates and around a quarter of the land in England and Wales changed hands. However, their influence in the countryside remained considerable. Many survived with substantial landholdings and their family seats largely intact into the inter-war years. They continued much as their ancestors had done in employing local people on a large scale in the rolling parklands, farmland and country houses. In total there might be

200–300 people in a district employed directly by the local estate, as well as many others, such as tradesmen, depending on the estate for their livelihood.

The influence of the lord (or squire) was felt most keenly in estate villages where everyone from the woodsman to the farmer was a tenant of the manor, living in a tied cottage or farm. Very often the lords owned whole villages on their estate. Estate village life had its advantages, as most of those villages were better built and better maintained than the cottage homes in villages where there was no squire or lord of the manor. Many of these estate or 'model' villages had been built in the nineteenth century. They were partly inspired by a paternalistic desire to see estate workers better housed and, as a result, more contented and loyal.

Landowners were also concerned to create a picturesque village outside the grand entrance gates leading towards the 'Big House' as a demonstration of family status, benevolence and good taste. Some of the most romantic and quaint villages were conceived by leading designers. These include the beautiful Blaise Hamlet near Bristol, designed by John Nash in 1810 for the workers of the Quaker estate owner, John Harford. Blaise Hamlet inspired numerous other picturesque villages, such as Selworthy in Somerset, Ilam in Derbyshire, Great Badminton in Gloucestershire and Sandy Land on the Bowood estate in Wiltshire.

Although these attractive cottages were not necessarily designed for the convenience of those who lived in them – the ceilings were often low and the small leaded windows made the rooms dark – they were undoubtedly superior to most other housing on offer to rural labourers. Some aristocrats, like the philanthropic first Duke of Westminster, devised grand building schemes. He built 360 cottages, eight schools, seven village halls, three churches and forty-eight farmhouses on his Cheshire estates around the family seat of Eaton Hall. Like many estate villages, the cottages bore the family coat of arms and initials.

The estate village of Ilam in Derbyshire (now Staffordshire).

In the early twentieth century there was less money for such grand building programmes but this patchwork of estate villages stretching across Britain survived. Most were built in a style determined by the local lord or squire and they shaped the local landscape profoundly. They were a permanent reminder to all who lived there of the power and wealth of their employers, and of their dependency on the family's good will and benevolence.

Although in the towns and cities people were becoming more and more politically conscious and critical of the class system, the countryside was slower to catch up and few questioned, at least in public, the private wealth of the landowner and the hierarchy of estate life. The landowner, usually from an old and respected family, could inspire loyalty and respect. But there was a touch of feudalism about the way he operated and some exercised firm control over the way locals lived their lives. Landowners who were staunch supporters of the Church, for example, expected their estate workers as well as servants to attend church. Villagers were too concerned not to cause offence to disoblige. The squire might well have also chosen the parson delivering the sermon to the congregation sitting away from the gentry in their specially segregated pews. During the shooting season tenant farmers were told to stop work temporarily in the fields or remove their cattle if it interfered with the shoot. Much depended on the whim of the individual landowner. Some tenants recall that all the doors of the houses would have to be painted a uniform colour; while the landowner provided the paint they provided the labour.

On the plus side, however, squires could be generous employers and made sure villagers found employment on the estate as gardeners, woodsmen, grooms and kennel staff. Many of the responsible squires took a well-meaning, if paternalistic, interest in the villagers' welfare. Some ladies regularly took their children to visit the cottagers in their homes with baskets of food and flowers and visited them when they were ill. During the shooting season the 'bag' might be shared out among tenants and estate workers. Christmas usually saw a party, abundant with food and drink, thrown for servants, cottagers and their children at the Big House or village hall. But a measure of humility and deference was expected. Schoolboys touched their forelocks and girls bowed gently and walked two steps backward after the Lord and Ladyship had presented them with their much-welcome present of a pair of boots or a choice of dress material. Pleasance Bett, born in 1915 on a country estate in Thornham, Norfolk, recalls Christmas as the highlight of the year for the tenants:

'Mother would give them a joint of meat which would be cut up according to the size of the family, numbered and put on a vast trestle table set up with a white cloth over it in the main barn. Jacob, our foreman, would call out the number and me or my brother Henry would find the right meat and the wife would come up, give a little bob and say, 'Thank you Master Henry or Miss Pleasance. Happy Christmas,' wrap the meat in a cloth and put it in her basket. It was probably the best meal they had in the year.'

Most of the youngsters born locally would go to work on the estate, either in the grounds or on the farms. Many were recruited through recommendation by the schoolmaster or through parents hearing of vacancies on the grapevine. The working life of some rural girls began behind the imposing park gates at the Big House. In the countryside, service was practically the only work available for girls, although elsewhere it was becoming increasingly unpopular in the inter-war years because of its low pay, low status and long hours. In rural counties like Norfolk and Oxfordshire a third or more of the girls working were in service.

A maid prepares tea for her mistress. For many country girls domestic service was the only option prior to the Second World War.

Nevertheless, there were certain advantages to working in service. A girl would gain valuable housekeeping skills, and after she had spent a few years with the gentry she might be considered more refined and eligible than a factory or farm girl. Also, unlike the lonely maid employed by a middle-class employer in a London town house, the servant working in a large country house had a certain status in terms of the reflected glory of being part of an aristocratic household or one whose pedigree dated back to the sixteenth century.

For many of the servants, however, the master and mistress remained distant figures. Most of life was lived out in the servant's hall under the beady and exacting eye of the butler, housekeeper and cook. Head servants ruled the house with a regimental discipline in order to attain the high standards demanded. There were no labour-saving devices and servants worked long and hard to keep the grand machine of the house – with its bedrooms, richly furnished reception rooms and maze-like service quarters – running like clockwork. Routines and timetables were unvarying. Servants had strictly prescribed roles from the scullery maid, whose kitchen duties included laboriously polishing copper jelly moulds and pans with silver sand and vinegar, to the butler who was entrusted with the wine, silver and keeping proper conduct at meals. Raymond Crees remembers his sometimes bizarre duties as a butler in the 1930s:

'I had to iron the newspapers every day after they had been read in the reception rooms. I had to collect up this Fleet Street confetti and take it down to the pressing room where I'd already heated up my iron ready – they weren't thermostatically controlled in those days – and I had to iron them and return them to the library and the morning room, and lay them on his Lordship's bureau in chronological order with just the banner headlines showing as though they'd just come out of Fleet Street.'

The rigid protocol so evident among their employers was mimicked behind the green baize door. Servants were extremely rank conscious and there was a strict hierarchy. Among the serried ranks might be the housekeeper, footmen, coachmen, tweenies (assistants to the cook and housemaid) and the humble hall boy. New recruits learnt how to be a servant by being a servant to the upper servants. They had to prepare their food, wash their dishes and clean their rooms. Cooks were always addressed as 'Mrs' whether married or not, and lady's maids were given the title of 'Miss' by those below them. Meals in the servants' hall were as formal as those in the dining room and servants sat around the table in order of rank.

Although servants had to – and did – know their place, many felt that the gentry were appreciative of their efforts and understood that without them the elaborate edifice of the Big

Ladies and gentlemen enjoying a hunt ball in Sevenoaks, Kent in 1935. During the inter-war years, foxhunting was in its heyday.

House would crumble. The landowners leant most heavily on their servants during the country house party, when their skills and hard graft meant the difference between success and failure. Visitors who might stay for a weekend or a few days meant more housework, more laundry and more gourmet meals to be served on lavish table settings.

Servants at Lord Dalmeny's Mentmore House in Whaddon Chase serve refreshments for huntsmen taking part in a 1924 meet.

    The country house party revolved around sport, and entertainment was practically non-stop. Keeping guests amused meant tennis, cricket, boating, and golf parties during long summer afternoons. Hunting and fishing were a regular feature of estate life during the winter months. The inter-war years were the heyday of fox hunting and it was regarded as a particularly thrilling sport for men and women alike. In 1922 there were twenty-five women for every one there had been in 1880 and the number of women masters had grown steadily. Glamorous bowler hats and breeches were *de rigueur*. Later the ladies would dress for dinner and they would be driven a few miles to a hunt ball where they danced until the early hours. Hunting was a fertile ground for romance and marriage. In the inter-war years the sport was attracting more and more 'new money' and marriage to the newly prosperous was a

Shooting was one of the most popular country pastimes of the English gentry in the 1920s. Shooting parties like this one at Eaton estate took place all over landed England.

way for the old landowners, beset by cash-flow problems, to survive in the countryside.

Shooting was also a popular, stylish social occasion. The Edwardian period has been called the 'golden age' of shooting, when plenty of men were used to participating three or four days a week throughout the season. No expense was spared. But shooting continued to flourish in the inter-war years. During the seasons of the various types of game there would be shooting weekends on estates all over the country. Landowners rivalled each other to produce the biggest bags of game on their estates. At the turn of the century, Sandringham was rearing 12,000 pheasants. These were in addition to the wild birds, partridges and hares already to be found on the estate. During a shoot at Hall Barn in Buckinghamshire in 1913, one of Lord Burnham's guests shot a staggering 3,937 pheasants.

The sport was a predominantly male pastime and few women were encouraged to participate. Country gentlemen set great store by these shoots and the sign of good marksmanship was to kill a pheasant directly in the head. But it was hardly a demanding sport. The hard work was being done behind the scenes in the coverts (thickets hiding game) by the estate gamekeepers with a team of beaters, usually made up of local men and boys. Led by the gamekeepers and wielding sticks they thrashed wildly at the bushes, clapping and hollering, to drive the pheasants rocketing skywards over the trees and towards the gentlemen's guns. A good shoot was judged by the height at which a pheasant could be shot. The higher the living target flew the better, and the gamekeeper who could make sure the birds flew high enjoyed a good reputation.

The gamekeeper was the man on whom the success of the shoot depended. Among his jobs was to keep the tenant farmer happy as he might be displeased if people traipsed over the working land and disregarded fundamental rules such as shutting gates. His primary role was to keep the estate well stocked with birds. Breeding was a very labour-intensive occupation. Brooding hens and their chicks, bred in coops in a field, had to be fed four times daily. Many hours had to be spent mixing large amounts of feed. He also needed to tackle predators, and the gamekeeper's gallows, with weasels, stoats and other vermin hanging from it, was both a display and a warning of his vigilance.

Shooting was the lifeblood of the winter season and there were strict game laws to protect deer, pheasant, partridge and other named foul. Poaching on estates was the most important rural crime against property. The countryman regarded the prized pheasants and other game as God's creatures; in the eyes of the law they were the landowner's property. Historically, poaching had long been a major source of tension between the gentry and villagers and estate workers, who were deferential by day but rebellious by night. In the early nineteenth century, steel mantraps, such as the dreaded 'iron wolf', and transportation had been used as deterrents for the poacher. Bloody affrays became the stuff of folklore, and the crafty poacher the hero of many a folk song. As late as 1915, the penalty for night poaching was three months' imprisonment for the first offence and seven years for a third. Not that the poacher could necessarily rely on the mercy or impartiality of the law, as the landowner or his estate agent might be sitting on the magistrate's bench.

Partridges are collected by liveried game-keepers at the Earl of Albemarle's shoot at Quidenham Hall, Norfolk in 1911.

Some, however, found the threat of imprisonment no deterrent. For the wily countryman, lured by the rolling fields, well-stocked rivers and secret woods, poaching was part and parcel of rural life. Skills were handed down from father to son and many reckoned themselves to be experts in the art of tickling trout, snaring rabbits and killing pheasants. One of the most important skills for night-time poaching was a thorough knowledge of the territory so as not to get lost under the cloak of darkness. A rough, windy night was perfect to dull the sound of footsteps when snaring an alert rabbit.

Much of the poaching was casual. Most men were driven, if not by poverty, at least by the desire to liven up the food on their family's plate at a time when the diet might consist of bread, a few vegetables, salt bacon and the occasional hard-earned Sunday joint. But class resentment and the illicit thrill of pitting his wits against the gamekeeper were also powerful pulls for the more rebellious-minded character. Many of the ill-gotten gains were hawked in the village pub or sold to their 'regulars', the tradesmen who supplied hotels and inns.

Gun in hand, a man prepares to poach pheasants in Essex.

It was not unheard of for women relatives, usually wives, to accompany the men. More often, however, they turned their skills to the preparation of the haul. Onions could disguise the strong smell of an illicit salmon wafting out of the cottage chimney and the resourceful housewife could find many uses for the oft-poached rabbit – from baking and stuffing to currying and stewing. But it was a fraught time waiting for the men to return safely from the woodlands and fields. Now ninety-three, Ruth Armstrong (then a farm labourer's wife from Wiltshire) kept her wits about her.

'My husband came rushing in and he said, "Oh, my goodness. The policeman and the keeper are after us and they know who we are." I said, "The only thing you can do is get upstairs, put your slippers on and ruffle your hair up so it looks like you've only just got up." I put the rabbits in the coalhole under the stairs and pushed coal over them with a shovel in case they came in.

There was a knock at the door and the keeper said, "Is your husband here?" I said he was just getting up so I called him, and he came down with the baby in her nightdress in his arms. The keeper said, "Well, that's funny because I was sure you were one of them."'

The gamekeeper was a powerful man at the time and his word on the estate was law. He was often more respected – and feared – than the village policeman. In 1911, there were twice as many gamekeepers in rural districts as policemen, and in agricultural counties such as Dorset and Suffolk there were twenty to thirty gamekeepers to every 10,000 inhabitants. In his bid to rear hundreds of pheasant chicks for the shoot, the gamekeeper already faced a 365-day war against vermin. In his eyes the poacher was also vermin to be eradicated. Often it was a game of cat and mouse between them – but who was cat and who mouse was not always certain. Poachers went to enormous lengths to keep themselves abreast of the gamekeeper's movements, checking the pub and his cottage before they set off. The gamekeeper, in turn, had his methods. He might stretch black cotton across vulnerable spots in the wood near the coverts and check to see whether it had broken. Another of his tricks was to deliberately smooth over the stretches of soft ground so that the telltale footprints of a poacher could be easily spotted.

The gamekeeper had a useful ally in the village policeman. He was invested with the powers to search a suspect in the country roads and lanes, and he didn't baulk at using them. He was also drafted in to help the gamekeeper patrol the unwieldy acres of land which could harbour a poacher. Sometimes, however, he could just as easily turn a blind eye. George Cook, now in his eighties, spent many a night during the 1920s helping his poacher father in the Essex woodlands, and in the early hours they would sort out the booty in their cottage.

'There would be a knock at the door. My father would say, "Go and see who that is," knowing full well it was the copper standing there with his helmet and cape on. "It's only me, Harry. I saw the light in the window and I was going back on patrol. I thought I'd come in and see what you've got for me tonight." The PC would look at the rabbits and pheasants lying on the floor and my father would ask what he fancied and then he'd help himself. He used to have a piece of string all ready in a sort of loop which he'd put round the pheasants' necks or rabbits' legs, put 'em under his arm and then roll his cape over to hide them.'

The poacher who lived in a tied cottage on an estate took a big risk. The ultimate threat was eviction. Landowners made sure, via their gamekeepers and agents, that their tenants were in no doubt as to what their punishment would be. For a tenant to lose his home meant that in all probability he and his family would have to uproot themselves and move to another village or even another area for work and accommodation. John Taylor and his family were evicted in 1931 from a Hampshire estate. The family already had poaching links but after his father, a stud groom, was accused of a crime against the manor employers the family was ordered to leave.

'I already had a place sorted out in my mind in the New Forest where the family could go to live, where there was a little stream and chestnut trees which had blown over so there was bags of firewood. The estate owners had got in touch with all the farmers miles around from here and told them that the Taylors were not to be trusted and not to employ us. Everywhere we turned it was, "No, we couldn't employ you, you're one of the Taylor gang." The people were tenants themselves and they weren't going to upset the landed gentry.'

Raymond Crees

Raymond Crees, born in 1917, was orphaned at a young age and brought up by his grand-parents in the village of Easebourne in Sussex. His first job at thirteen was as a hall boy-cum-pantry boy in a country house with twenty-five servants, and the splendour and glamour inside made a big impression on him. Now eighty-two, he lives in Surrey.

I would ring the servant's gong, which was a totally different tone to the gentry's gong, so that they could leave their work upstairs and come down to the servants' hall. I'd bring the food in and everyone would stand behind their chairs, hands behind their backs, waiting for the coming up of his lordship, the butler. He would come in and scan us with a rather supercilious look on his face, as though we'd just crawled out from under a green stone, and then when he sat down we could sit down.

A butler presides over a dinner party in the late 1930s. Standing to attention throughout the long meals was second nature for a butler and his footmen.

I made a dreadful **faux pas** *the very first day I was there. Coming from very poor circumstances I couldn't help ploughing through this delicious food. I noticed that everyone else had stopped eating. They hadn't finished their food but the butler had finished, and so to recognise this fact we had to put down our knives and forks and in his own good time he would rise, check his gold watch and leave the servants' hall. For some obscure reason – this went on right through the hierarchy of the big houses – the housekeepers and lady's maids all trooped out behind the butler down many corridors to a little room called the 'pug's parlour' and had their second course.*

The butler was an exacting man. In the morning I had to scrub the steps outside the billiard room, the reading-room and the library, and then heave up a huge rubber mat on the parquet flooring by the front doors and scrub underneath. Well, of course, with breakfast beckoning a boy of thirteen, I sometimes used to skip that. The butler would call the footman who would stand on the doorstep holding a basin of water. He'd make a signal to the footman who passed him a pair of white cotton gloves, which he put on. He would dangle a digit in the water and prod his sausage-like finger down through the holes in this rubber mat. If there was dust on the end of the glove he knew I hadn't cleaned underneath and so I had to miss my breakfast and wait 'til lunchtime.

About a month after I was there the butler called me into the pantry and told me that he could no longer bellow 'Raymond' down the various corridors searching for me. From that moment onwards I was rechristened 'John' because Raymond was far too grand a name for a servant. I was fiercely angry about this but I gradually adjusted myself to the new name.

In the mornings I had to spend four hours at least cleaning and polishing the silver in the butler's pantry. As lunch was six courses and dinner was eight courses and there were nearly always twenty or twenty-four people to dinner, you can imagine the silverware that was fed through to me. Her Ladyship was so strict that if, for instance, a spoon had a scratch on it, she would send it back and I had to clean it, wearing down the silver until it was level with the scratch and thus eliminate that scratch.

I was working all the hours God created so I was always hungry. When the trolley used to come out from behind the green baize door, my job was to take it to the pantry and sort out all the silver dishes and anyone's uneaten food and take it back to the kitchen. This was my ploy: I knew that the butler would be in the dining room with his henchmen so I used to wheel the trolley into his pantry, open one of the many cupboard doors, stand behind one and eat my way to paradise with perhaps a pork

Kitchen staff like these at Keele Hall, Staffordshire (c.1900) spent hours arduously preparing the lavish dishes consumed by the upper classes.

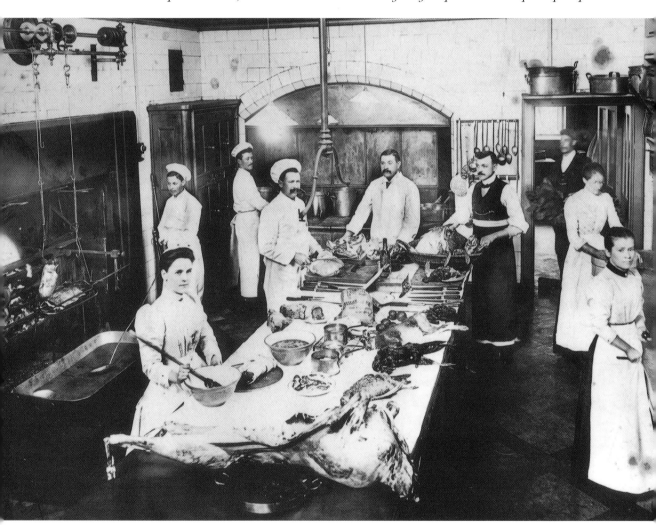

chop, venison or hare cooked in port wine. Had the butler come by he would have seen my legs below the level of the door and assumed I was putting stuff away. This is the way I got my extra food, my extra dynamite if you like, to keep me going for the next long period of time before I could go to bed.

I'd never seen a pineapple before (they grew their own on the estate) and this one night there was a pineapple among the different sweets on the gentry's trolley. The cook, in her wisdom, had sliced off the top, scooped out all the flesh inside and the beauty of it was that she had then poured lavish amounts of the finest liqueurs – green and yellow chartreuse – into the bottom. She'd topped it up with chopped peaches, nectarines and grapes and put the lid on top and then piped cream to represent the leaves of a pineapple. There was a lot of it left after dinner so I took it to the butler's pantry and picking up the largest spoon I could find, I started attacking the forbidden fruit. Before long I was dredging out these lovely, strong liqueurs from the bottom. At thirteen years old it was more than flesh and blood could stand.

As I wheeled the trolley back to the kitchen it was ricocheting off the walls. All the servants and even her Ladyship would never, ever cross the threshold of the kitchen without knocking. But I was on cloud nine and just used my trolley as a battering ram and forced the door open. I knocked over a large pile of tins which flew across the kitchen like a flock of geese in a great cacophony and I caught the cook red-handed, drunk as a fiddler, sitting in an armchair in the kitchen, toasting her toes by the fire and swigging out of a bottle of cooking sherry. The expletives that fell from that lady's lips that night!

The next morning the butler said to me, 'Now! Her Ladyship wishes to see you in the drawing room.' He virtually frog-marched me across and tapped on the door and disappeared. A very stern voice said, 'Come in.' There was her Ladyship lying on a chaise longue and between her two fingers was a long onyx cigarette holder with a cigarette stuffed in the end. The smoke was curling lazily to the ceiling and she was looking over the top of a pair of half-rimmed glasses. 'Are you getting enough to eat, John?' Like a fool, I grinned all over my face and said, 'Yes, thank you, my Lady.' Then she turned up the heat and said, 'Why, if you are getting sufficient to eat, did you have the temerity, the audacity, to consume the remainder of the pineapple, which his Lordship and I were going to have for lunch today?' I felt lower than the pile in the carpet.

When I became a footman my salary went up by £2 per annum. My livery was tailor-made. It consisted of a long, heavily quilted coat – green velvet with thirty-two silver buttons with the armorial bearings of the house on them – and a wasp waistcoat, so-called because it was banded yellow and black. I also wore thick trousers and a stiff boiled shirt with a wing collar and a bow tie. In the summer we footmen had a way of combating this rather uncomfortable garb by going down to the village and buying what was known in the trade as a 'dickey'. It was made of paper and was a false *shirtfront fastened around my waist with a piece of elastic. Consequently my arms and back were bare, much more comfortable in the high summer. The final illusion was one-penny cardboard cuffs slipped into the sleeves of my livery so that when they shot up while serving at the table, her Ladyship would think I was wearing a well-laundered shirt as we were forbidden to wear this.*

When any branch of royalty used to come to dinner, we wore a frock coat, velvet breeches, stockings, buckled shoes, powdered wigs and white gloves, almost like the Scarlet Pimpernel age. The footmen were chosen for being almost the same height, but some of them had skinny legs and, so her Lady didn't have to see these pieces of white celery sticking out of the ends of the breeches, the village tailor would make cardboard 'calves' we could stick in our stockings.

There was a very, very rigid etiquette that had to be followed and everything worked to a pattern. Punctuality was a terrific thing, which had to be observed. There was a clock winder who came from the village once a week and wound up all the clocks, of which there were many, French and Hungarian, all sorts. Dinner had to be served at eight o'clock in the dining room but prior to that at 7.15pm the dressing gong was sounded by the butler so that the people standing around drinking pink gins and sherry could go up to their boudoir and dress in their full tails.

The butler would go across to the dining room doors, pause, open them and in his very sepulchral voice say, 'Dinner is served, my Lady.' There were two footmen already in the dining room to push the chairs under the bottoms of the more important people. The other two footmen, which quite often included myself, flanked the entrance into the dining room and then every gentleman would offer his arm to the nearest lady in the drawing room and escort her in this beautiful manner.

We always served on the left and always the guest of honour first, going around the table with the lesser guests coming last. After each course was finished it would be loaded on to the trolley for the hall boy to take back to the kitchen. In the interim we had to stand like sentinels at the end of the dining room, with the butler keeping his beady eye on us, waiting for the next course to be delivered.

My most dreadful time serving dinner was when I was taking in these Georgian sauceboats on a silver tray. The last person to be served was, in my young country boy's eyes, the most gorgeous, glamorous-looking young woman, wearing the lowest-cut evening frock I'd ever seen in my life. As she started taking the sauce out of the boat I was looking down the front of her dress and began to lose control of my right hand and tilted the boat. Before I knew what was happening there was gravy dripping down the back of her beautiful dress. Then she did something which was totally taboo in those days. She just left the table and went upstairs, changed her frock and came down. She was so good to me: she played her part extremely well, because she knew that I would be for the high jump if my misdemeanour was discovered.

Cyril Rice

Born in 1916, Cyril Rice grew up in mid-Wales in the village of Cwmbach, Welsh for 'little valley'. His father rented a smallholding and was a carpenter on the large estate where they lived. Cyril became a painter and decorator, a job he kept up all his life until his retirement. He lives in Dyfed.

A teenage Cyril Rice takes a dip in the river.

The butler at the big house asked my parents, 'Would your boy come and work as a hall boy? He'd fit in nicely.' Well, I didn't want to be a blooming hall boy. It wasn't my type of life at all but you didn't say no.

Life was so restricted. When the Lady of the house came round I had to touch my cap and say, 'Good morning, Madam,' or 'Good afternoon, Madam.' No matter how many times you met her, it was 'three bags full, Madam'. You had to be up at half-past six in the morning, stoking the boilers up for the hot water and baths. Then when other lads were out enjoying themselves in the evening, well, there you were, waiting on the table every night. They had a six-course dinner, see, and you had to do all the washing-up and polish all the glassware and chamois all the silver. You finished at about eleven o'clock at night.

Once when they were entertaining, just as the gentlemen were going into the billiard room, a blinking rat run across the hall. The mistress was very upset about it and she discussed it with Wall, the butler. He knew I was pretty well versed in country lore so he said that I'd get a shilling for every rat I trapped. There was a rat infestation nearby and they were coming up to the big house, which was pretty ancient. I set lots of traps. Every morning the mistress would come along to the kitchen to give her orders to the cook. She'd say, 'Morning, Cyril, any rats this morning?'

'Yes, Madam, two rats.'

'Very good Cyril; two shillings.'

I must admit, I wasn't entirely honest. At our smallholding at home we had a few rats about the cowshed and pig sheds and me father was trapping them. When it came to my half-day I'd go home, slip them up in a bag and take them back and pretend I'd caught them there to get more money. I made a lot more in a few days than on a month's wages.

Because most of their business interests were in shipping, every two months the owners would go to London, and then from London to Antwerp and maybe be away for a fortnight. Of course, then I used to do some poaching. You had to be careful about not being seen because some of the workmen on the estate were crawlers and they wouldn't have been above tipping off the toffs.

The stuff I poached I took home to enliven our table. We didn't have much meat except for salt bacon and you got a bit tired of that. Pheasants and salmon were delicacies and the icing on the cake, weren't they? They were so mouth-watering because the choice of meals was so limited. Salmon or roast pheasant with the stuffing and the breadcrumbs and the gravy, and perhaps Brussels sprouts or peas, it was such a treat.

Of course, Mum was nervous because she was even more in awe of the toffs than what I was. I was, well, a bit resentful of them to tell you the honest truth. She'd say, 'I shan't touch it, I won't touch it, I will not eat it.' But she tucked in the same as the rest of us when it was cooked. While we were frying salmon I'd whipped out of the river, we'd burn a few chicken feathers to camouflage the fish smell so if anybody went by they wouldn't know. If word got back that you were feasting on salmon, oh blimey, that would have been the end of the world. With Mum, it wasn't a case of conscience because Mum felt the same as me, that if there was a God he had put things on earth for everybody, like the rain which falls from the sky. Why shouldn't we be entitled to what was on the land rather than just a few moneyed people who were able to buy all that land? The fear with my mum was if I was discovered my father would be out of his job and we'd be without a roof over our heads.

Counting the kill at Stonor Park, Henley-on-Thames in 1911. Land-owners hoped to outdo each other with the biggest bags of game on their estate.

I stuck the job for two years but I was pretty cheesed off. It was no life for a young lad. You had one half-day a week off but you had to wash up the lunch things. By the time you were free to leave it was half-past two and you had to be in at half-past nine. When I left that was a very, very black mark. My wages was 10s a month [50p] and the Lady of the house told the butler to tell me that if I withdrew my notice they'd increase my wages to 12s 6d a month, which wasn't by any means a fortune.

I worked as a painter and decorator, but quite often the weather wasn't suitable and I had spells of unemployment. I had to poach to help things along and when my father died I was virtually the breadwinner, and I had a sister at home who was blind and I had to support her. I got a bit more businesslike with the poaching.

When we'd do the river there would be several boys who I had taught a bit of country craft to. We'd walk up and down the river and stake it out. You'd come to a ford where the water wasn't so deep across and that's the place where the salmon would come up to spawn. Well, one lad kept watch, well-hid in the bushes, while the rest of us would catch a salmon.

With pheasants you knew pretty well what wood and coverts the pheasants all congregated in because the keepers were feeding them with corn every day, just like chickens, ready for the toffs and beaters to come for the shoot. Moonlight was no good because the pheasants saw you before you saw them and that was it. It had to be a starlit night. You'd be creeping along and see the pheasants silhouetted against the stars up in the branches and they'd be craning their necks. Then you'd get your gun, point the barrel and shoot them in the head. You'd pop as many as two or three pheasants and then you'd strike off in another direction. You had to keep your ear open because you knew the keeper would be out around somewhere.

I was able to get £1 a pheasant and that was a lot of money. There were two places I could sell them; one supplied hotels in the area with game. It would be wrong to say that poaching was all poverty-driven. Part of it was the thrill and part of it was that you were giving these old toffs you had to doff off your cap to, their come-uppance.

Once the head keeper said to me, 'Look Cyril, if you should happen to be not working on such and such a day, come beating during the shoot.' Well, I went beating all this day. Before lunch even they'd shot 400 pheasants. When the evening came we were all gathered there because they used to give birds out to the tenants and the workmen. The mistress was calling out the names. I was still standing there and my name hadn't been called. Well, fair play to the keeper, he walked up to the heap and picked up a brace.

The master said, 'Price, what are you doing with those birds, man?'

'Well, sir,' he said, 'Mrs Rice's son hasn't been called yet.'

'If the mistress had intended to give Mrs Rice a brace she would have called her name. Put them back down at once man.'

And that was it. I think it was because I'd had the audacity to leave them as a hall boy. I was bound to feel resentful. I was in such a fret that night that I went out and shot six pheasants out of sheer temper and got away with it. From then on, oh, God, I was killing pheasants right, left and centre.

It was the buzz, see. If you'd had heavy rain and then the weather dried off and it was a little bit frosty, well, that was lovely. You'd be wading through the river and get the salmon in sacks. I'd be walking home across the field so excited that I didn't feel the cold even though my trousers would be frozen stiff as a board. It was just the excitement in your blood.

I never got caught. I remember one gamekeeper stopping me. I was just about to go to work and he said, 'Damn you, Cyril Rice. I know you shoot bloody pheasants but I can't catch you.' Of course, I swore blind I never did it. Oh, God, there would be times when you was scared to death. One of the reasons I never got caught was I was an extremely fast runner. The keepers were nearly double my size, a bit more cumbersome, and couldn't keep up. I'd take a short cut, jump over a stile, vault over a gate. That, and fright, lent speed to my wings.

Lady Maureen Fellowes

Lady Maureen Fellowes, the daughter of the Earl of Gainsborough, was born in 1917 and grew up on Exton Park, an estate of some 6,000 acres in Rutland. Her grandfather and father died within fifteen months of each other in the late Twenties and the double death duties forced her mother to rent out their country house for a few years until their return before the war. Lady Maureen, twice married and now a widow, lives in Gloucestershire.

The real joy of growing up on a lovely, big estate for me was just being able to roam about, sort of wild, and do what I liked. You could go anywhere you wanted, play anywhere you wanted. You could go down the park and have a picnic. You might climb the trees and perhaps have a Wendy house in them. You could just be very free and easy and simple. My grandfather was an ornithologist [studied birds and their behaviour] so he collected wild flowers and had a few eggs that he used to teach us about.

My grandparents and aunt and uncle did look after the villagers. I gather now that the villagers thought my grandmother, Lady Gainsborough, was very stiff and expected all the children to curtsey to her and they all made fun of her in the end. But my parents entered into everything and were very popular. My mother made friends with them all and brought us up like that. The villagers attributed that to the fact that my mother was American. I don't think it was only because she was American because I can remember my aunt was very keen on all the village people too.

It was a sort of miniature life of its own in the village and on the estate, which went on all over England in those days. If there was a village fête or a bazaar or dance we all went to it. We used to have fishing competitions on the lake in the estate with all the village people coming up. Everything really that needed to be done on the estate could be done by people from the village. I mean there were carpenters, plumbers, painters and the odd job man, everyone.

Our servants were nearly all Irish because my grandmother was Irish and she imported all these girls to give them jobs because they were so poor. All down the

Lady Maureen Fellowes as a 'deb's delight' in the 1930s. Like all well-bred daughters of the gentry she was presented at court to the King and Queen.

Debutantes at Dorchester Hotel in 1931. At the end of the London season in July, mothers with daughters of marriageable age embarked on a round of visits to country houses in the hope of making a match with an eligible young man.

passage by the back stairs in the big houses there were rows of bells which dingled and dangled when you pulled the strings. The servants would go and look and see which bell had rung and they'd know if it was the drawing room, or the study or the bedrooms. When you finished tea and had eaten all the cakes and the cucumber sandwiches, then you rang the bell for them to clear all the tea away. You pulled the bell if the firewood was getting low to ask them to put the last logs on the fire and fill up the fire baskets with more logs.

There was always plenty to eat. We were self-sufficient on the estate. We had fresh vegetables from the kitchen garden, which was enormous, and fresh eggs, milk and cream from the home farm. At one-thirty on the dot you had a three-course lunch. For dinner it was always this wretched soup to start with, which you called an entrée. Then you had the main course which was always meat, perhaps chicken or game, with masses of vegetables and then a fully-fledged pudding. Then you had a savoury, which was composed of all sorts of things like scrambled egg on toast with anchovies on top or grilled kidneys, and there were all different kinds of cheese.

I came out in 1935. There were so many debutantes that year, it was all very strictly arranged. We were presented at court to the King and Queen and all the girls that year became friends if you liked them. Every night we had a dance. You bought lovely materials, real silk velvet and real taffeta, real silk tulle. Everybody found a little dressmaker that made them up. I think they cost about £12 or £14 at the most. It was brand new and nobody had one like it because it was made at home. I suppose I had about twelve dresses. Every woman had her own lady's maid and she mended and pressed the clothes, ironed and hung them up and laid them out. When my mother's lady's maid had done all my mother's things she would come in and see me.

My mother taught me that if you had a dinner party you had to get the precedence right. Dukes obviously came top. If you got Lady so-and-so and she was the Duke's daughter she went on the right of the leading man. If you had two Dukes' daughters you had to look up which was the oldest Duke.

You didn't think, 'I'm the leading lady, I'm very grand,' you just got on with it. You just thought about what dress you were going to wear and which men you were going to dance with. There were probably about fourteen dances in the evening and you wrote down the names of the boys whom you were going to dance with. Boys used to ring you up before you went to the dinner party and say, 'Will you write it down and put it in your bag – I'll have dance number five.' So you went off with all these arranged beforehand so that sometimes you could say to the boys you didn't want to dance with, 'I'm awfully sorry. I know you're asking me out of politeness but my card's all booked up so I can't dance with you.' You had to flirt with your eyes. I had a friend who said, 'Will you teach me to flirt?' and I said, 'No, my dear girl, you can't teach people to flirt. You just flirt or you don't flirt. You talk with your eyes.'

After the first season when you'd kept all the rules, you could go to dances, often without a mother, so you didn't have to have your chaperone any more. They did used to sit around, you see, grimly staring at you dancing around the ballroom, so you couldn't do much to get into trouble. My mother was pretty good at telling me what to do and what not to do, she was very worldly. She could tell you how to get the best fun out of everything without falling into the pitfalls. We had boundaries. Holding hands, yes, but not a lot of kissing at all, really, and certainly not a lot of cuddling or canoodling. We were very strictly brought up. I wasn't going to get in with the fast girls, you see; they would go a bit further and that ended up in the bedrooms.

I suppose some people tried to push their daughters into marriage; my mother didn't do that at all. She was a very good hostess and we had a large amount of people to choose from but she didn't put pressure on me, luckily.

The first boy who proposed to me was very annoyed because he said that I had led him up the garden path. His name was Joe and they were a very old county family who lived in a lovely old house on the Wye on the borders of Wales near Monmouth. I was only carrying on with my flirtatious ways, which I thought quite harmless, but he read more into it. He proposed in the middle of supper at a dance, which I didn't think was particularly romantic to start with. He sort of suddenly clutched my hand and said, 'Wouldn't it be lovely if we were married?' I recoiled in horror and said, 'No, it wouldn't be lovely at all, I've got no intention of getting married.' I was very apologetic but I was perfectly happy with my life. I was only just nineteen. I said to him, 'Don't you realise this is the age you have a good time, that's what we're here to have.' We were frivolous in those days. So he went off disgusted and I went off and had a good time. But we remained good friends.

The country house parties were a bit intimidating unless you really knew the people very well. We were all terribly nervous, thinking, 'Oh, we've got to go and stay with this Lady so-and-so or Lord so-and-so, what are they going to be like?' We always used to go by train in those days and our maids bought all the tickets and did all those sorts of things. You were treated like an idiot, as though you couldn't do anything for yourself. They packed our clothes and unpacked our clothes and got us off the train in one piece and back on again. When you got to the actual house you were going to stay in, you had to start being on your own and going down and taking part. We often smoked when we didn't want to because we were nervous and wanted to do something with our hands. Someone would offer you a cigarette and then light it for you and that would start a conversation; that sort of broke the ice.

Precedence came up again. Lady Winifred, she was the Duke of Norfolk's sister, had the best room. I was the Earl's daughter so I had the next best room. Generally we were in rooms next to each other which was nice. Lady Winifred often took her nanny with her and I took the head parlour maid and she used to be my lady's maid. The younger

ones never knew how to behave – didn't enjoy it – so we used to take the head servants because they enjoyed all the precedence and all the kind of paraphernalia. The rank you had as a Duke's daughter or an Earl's daughter meant the servants carried the same rank as you had below stairs. Lady Winifred's old nanny would be taken first into the still room [the pantry] on the arm of the butler. My one would follow with whoever was next. It was very formalised but we took an awful lot of it for granted. It was a sort of system, wasn't it?

The aristocracy or whoever were the leading members of the family, they used to talk about the most extraordinary things at mealtimes in front of the servants that you would never have thought that they would have wanted to. They'd come out with every sort of scandal as if the wretched servants were part of the furniture.

In some of the big country houses there were very few bathrooms so we would go into all the hipbaths that you now see in films. Big brass cans of hot water were brought in and in the very posh country houses they all had the crests and the monograms on these wretched things they brought the water in. They were quite heavy and some of these young girls that had to bring them; one felt quite sorry for them.

It seemed like the world would go on forever. Then the war came and it was never the same again. It dawned on you that it was finished. In the big house where we lived in Rutland we had all these different servants, eight, nine, ten, eleven servants, all doing different things. After the war we just had one couple and dailies who came in and cleaned from the village. So you had to be much more practical yourself and not make trouble and not think that everything was going to be done for you. You had to look after your own things, hang up your own clothes because it had to be. It changed pretty radically.

David Spreckley

David Spreckley was born in 1915, the year his mother, sister and father, a captain in the Gurkha regiment, were all drowned in a troop ship that was torpedoed. David escaped because he was too ill to travel and had stayed with his nanny. He was adopted by a wealthy cousin and raised on a 2,000-acre Sussex estate. David was a Conscientious Objector during the war and afterwards became a bookseller promoting organic farming and a Labour, and then Liberal, councillor in Huntingdon.

My father was called the Lord of the Manor. I don't think that there was anything official about that, he had just sort of taken it upon himself. So when we walked around the village all the men took their caps off. The women would bow gently. This deference was something I accepted as being the way life was ordained for me. In those days one would have used the phrase 'God given'.

When we went to church we had our own pew which nobody else would dare to sit on. When the service was over we were expected to go out first. People stood outside and touched their caps. My mother would make small talk with them like Lady Bountiful. I remember vividly her doing the gracious lady act to a dear man, when he farted! She didn't say anything but gently backed away. I enjoyed the memory all my life.

Hunt balls like this one at Lylney Hall, Pottierwick in 1934 often saw romance blossom between huntsmen and women.

The rural hierarchy was an absolute fixture. There was the labourer, the farm carter, the pig man or cow man and that was where he would stay the rest of his life. The village butcher was a level above the manual workers. All these levels were known to us and we were very careful that we got the levels right in the way we addressed them. There would be a level above us. A few miles away there was a family in an even bigger house where they had a footman and the man of the house was a 'Sir'. My parents were acutely aware that they hadn't reached that level, even though they went there for dances.

We had this hierarchy of servants and we treated them rather differently. The servants certainly were not friends. I was always alluded to as Master David by everybody and I addressed them with their Christian names except for Walters, the butler, Mrs Reynolds, the cook, and the head gardener, who was called Mr Wright. The one exception was the gamekeeper, Joe. I didn't like my father and Joe really became a substitute father. He took me out, taught me how to shoot and taught me a lot about the land, livestock and the countryside too. I learnt from him and he was a friend.

I think I was completely spoilt by this way of life. I should think I was a very unpleasant boy towards the servants in the way I ordered them about. For instance, we had a groom who lived in one of the lodges and he had a son called Hugh, who was about my age. Poor Hugh had to come out and play some game with me whenever I wanted him to. I would just go there whether he was having his tea or anything else and say to his mother, 'Can Hugh come out to play?' He'd have to come and we'd go on a boat on a little pond or we played tennis or croquet or golf. It was obvious that he was told to make sure that he usually lost the game. I don't think I was aware of that at the time, but with hindsight I can see it was happening.

Looking back, the meals we had were absolutely amazing. We ate the most incredible amount. Breakfast was always on the sideboard. There would be a choice of three dishes: kedgeree, liver and bacon, eggs and bacon. Before that we'd have cereal and after toast and a choice of three marmalades. At one o'clock we would have a three-course lunch, and then at half past four there was tea with cucumber sandwiches and a choice of three different cakes. The evening meal would again be at least three courses and we ate it all. Oh, I enjoyed the food. How I got all that stuff through my little tummy I cannot imagine, but we did that every day. We were always constipated.

There was certainly a complete etiquette of the food. At lunch and dinner we were served by the butler and the parlour maid. The butler would serve one course, the main meat course perhaps, and the parlour maid would come round with the vegetables. The evening meal was a full dress occasion. I always put my dinner jacket on when I got old enough. My parents were always in evening dress. We had to do it every night of our lives. I didn't find it oppressive because I didn't know any alternative.

We had that system of old-fashioned tinkling bells in various rooms and that it is the way that the servants were summoned – 'summonsed' was the operative word.

They would be asked to bring tea, which would be taken in the library at six o'clock, and they would be asked to bring the sherry or possibly the daily papers. The paper always arrived every day at eight o'clock even though we were miles out in the country. As soon as I got beyond prep school age, I was given the parlour maid as my sort of valet and she looked after my clothes and laid them out for me every day.

Every morning of my life we had prayers before breakfast except Sunday when we went to church. The servants would all come in one by one and sit on chairs all around the edges of the dining room. My father sat at the big table with my mother on one side and me on the other with a Bible in front of him and he would read something from it. Walters, the butler, would come in last and every day he did exactly the same thing: he would pick up the brass door stop that was holding the dining room door open, close the door, put down the brass stop, pull out a chair, flip up his little tails from his coat

Huntsmen from the Devon and Somerset Hounds set off for the chase in 1926.

and sit down. This dear little butler, he was a very small man. One of his jobs was when I came back from hunting he would run me a mustard bath and take my muddy boots off. Now, taking off the boots meant that he turned his back; me, I put one boot up between his legs and put my other foot on his backside and pushed.

I started riding at the age of five. I used to go hunting at least twice a week. At the age of eight I was blooded. They had just killed a fox and I was called up to the master of the hounds, sitting on his horse. He passed the fox to someone on the ground who took a knife and cut the head off and handed it back to the master. I was sitting on my pony alongside. Then he dipped his fingers into the back of the severed head, covered them in blood, leant over and smeared my face with the blood. Then I was a real huntsman! I felt great pride and excitement. I loved it. I enjoyed the skill of riding and galloping and jumping over fences. Oh, it's very thrilling. In those days, on the hunt we did a tremendous amount of damage to the farms and the farmers got very small compensation. We'd chew the farms up no end and break down the fences. Of course, all the local boys and sometimes old people as well would stand at the gates and open and close them because cattle were probably in the fields. We would carry a pocket full of small change, which we dispensed for opening the gate.

In 1935, I joined the Royal Dragoons, the highest regiment after the Household Cavalry, stationed in India. It was there I began to get doubts about the righteousness of the life I was leading. I became disgusted with the whole set-up of the British Empire and British way of life. I resigned my commission and took my charger. I went back to

The Bicester hunt in the 1900s. Villagers would gather to catch the coins thrown to them by the huntsmen for opening the gates.

the stately home where I lived to tell my parents. I don't remember any details; I tried to forget it because it wasn't very pleasant. They didn't like it but they couldn't cut me off without a penny because my real father had left a certain amount for me when I became twenty-one. It was enough for me to live on for a few years, but as regards the estate and everything else, I was simply cut out. I never lived in that house again.

I thought I would emulate William Cobbett and ride around England on the horse by myself. I did this for three months. I covered 1,200 miles in a circle round the south country, up through Wales and up to York and down the other side. It was the law then that any pub that had a stable had to put up horses so I would stay in these little pubs. My problem had been that in my fragile, protected life all my relationships with people, particularly in the country, were as servants or as manual workers. Once I got on to my horse and got into these villages I found that they were equal human beings and very friendly and it did me a hell of a lot of good. One of the things that impressed me was the way that the country people seemed so very happy in their lives. Oh, sure they were poor, but they didn't behave as though they were poor. I had some wonderful encounters and found the most wonderful hospitality. Once I was invited to stay with a Welsh farmer. They gave me their local scrumpy which was so strong, about 20 per cent proof, that I absolutely passed out and was in bed all the next day.

David Spreckley rejected his privileged life in 1936 to begin a 'rural ride' around England's countryside.

Norman Mursell

Born in 1914, Norman was brought up in Bembridge on the Isle of Wight. He became an underkeeper on the Duke of Westminster's Eaton estate at the age of fourteen and three years later he became a gamekeeper. After the Second World War, Norman was appointed head keeper, which lasted until he retired in 1979. He lives with his wife in the same tied cottage in the estate village of Aldford in Cheshire that he lived in when he began work.

At the crack of dawn the beaters and keepers used to meet outside the hall, which was a very large residence with big, long golden gates, a bit like Buckingham Palace from a distance. And the keepers would be in their livery: the senior ones with a green velvet coat, green velvet waistcoat with brass buttons with the Grosvenor crest, and white breeches. They all wore the old hard bowler hat and the head keeper had that much gold braid round it you had a job to see the top of it. The junior ones just had one piece of braid round it. These hundred beaters, all employees of the estate, they were on parade and wore white smocks and a red bush hat, a leather belt around the hat and brown leather leggings. It was a spectacular sight, just as the sun was coming up all these colours in front of the golden gates. I did feel proud of it.

The first year I was at Eaton I was the lad carrying the cartridge for the Duke's gun loader. Mr Winston Churchill, as he was in those days, was the next gun about forty yards away. He shot a very high pheasant and the Duke saw it. He said, 'Mursell, go and get that bird and pull a tail feather out and stick it in Winston's hat.' So I got the pheasant and watched for my opportunity. I said, 'Excuse me, sir, his Grace wants me to stick this feather in your hat.' I pulled this tail feather out and he looked at me and said, 'You'd better do that then, lad, hadn't you?' And I did.

They would probably only have three, four, maybe five days shooting through the winter and they wanted good days, they wanted to entertain their friends. At Eaton in pre-war days there were twenty gamekeepers and we used to rear about 20,000 pheasants. We used to rear a few more just to be on the safe side but on top of that we had to rear partridge and wild duck. Driving pheasants over guns was a very complicated business because you had, say, eight guns stretched out with approximately thirty-five to forty yards between them, and you had to do your best to get them fairly even so they all got a reasonable amount of shooting. We were fortunate because the beaters were estate employees and many had been beating for years and they knew exactly what to do. It was a culmination of about nine months' work, so we did our very, very best to ensure that it was as near perfect as possible. Nobody was allowed to take tips from the guests that were shooting there but at Christmas his Grace usually sent us a short little note with, perhaps, a £5 note in it in connection with the shooting that season. Five pounds was a lot of money in those days – wages were £2 a week.

Norman Mursell as a young gamekeeper on the Eaton estate in Cheshire before the Second World War.

The Duke of Westminster's main occupation during the winter was shooting of all descriptions. He was very fond of pheasant shooting, partridge shooting, grouse shooting and, in particular, snipe shooting. He'd spend other parts of the year very largely yachting because in those days he used to run two yachts, one in Scotland and the other in the Mediterranean, so he did a lot of entertaining as well. It was accepted by everybody that there were wealthy people that followed no work of any description and there were the working classes.

There was one thing about the people with a lot of money that didn't actually work; they spent a deuce of an amount in employing these other people. In the 1930s people were glad to have a job anyway, and if these rich people who provided the work were good people there was no feeling against them having a lot. There was a lot of prestige working on an estate like the Eaton estate. They were such good employers but it was the general atmosphere that was the main thing. Everybody was loyal to the Duke. If anything needed doing it didn't matter what time of the day or night it was, they did do it and wouldn't even think about the extra pay.

Most of the large estates between the wars were run as sporting estates; they weren't all that concerned about the farming side of it. Of course, it was very important indeed to ensure that there was no poaching, particularly pheasant poaching.

Oh, we detested the pheasant poachers because they were tending to destroy our long hard labours for many months and we weren't going to have that. But we were fortunate as we had twenty keepers and we used to have a rota so that there was somebody on duty every hour of the darkness. I could tell ninety-nine times in a hundred if anybody or anything had been in the wood. They'd leave a mark of some sort, even if it was only a flattened piece of grass. You had to have a photographic mind. If you saw a footprint you'd stare at it until you remembered it. In those days they used to wear a lot of nail boots and there might be a nail missing or it might be worn on one side a bit more than on the other. When you were around and about talking to various people, say a farm worker, you'd look at his foot mark and think, 'Ah, that's the bloke that has been there.' Sometimes you felt like a wildlife detective.

Prior to a pheasant shoot Norman Mursell takes charge of the beaters, who were all employees of the Eaton estate.

If there was a potential poacher in the woods we had a gun with us and we'd discharge two barrels rapidly – bang, bang – which was the indication that we needed help and the other keeper would come as quickly as possible in the direction that he'd heard the shot. At times I suppose I felt a bit frightened if there was more than one of them. But if there was one it didn't bother me because I always had a stick. As long as you didn't lose your temper you were the boss and you just said, 'Are you coming quietly because I've got a stick here and I know what to do with it,' and they usually gave in. What was a great help to us was we knew most of the local poachers and once we got to them we would call them by name and they knew it would just be a waste of time trying to get away. It was a grand feeling when you got a poacher cornered and nabbed him because you had it in your mind, 'Well, I beat that devil this time. He might have got away with it once or twice but he hasn't got away with it this time.' No doubt they did get away with it occasionally, but on a well-keepered estate not very often.

Once we were netting rabbits and I saw a bloke setting a net. I knew the poacher's call sign and I made it, 'tck, tck tck' quietly, and he answered. Of course he walked straight up to me so I told him who I was and took all the nets off him and the two others with him. I said to my mate, 'I don't suppose that there will be anybody else about tonight,' so we went into one of the cabins and we sat down and had a smoke. Then as we made our way back I went to have a look at this one particular place where poachers used to put their bikes. As I was walking by this big tree with a holly bush around it I went 'tck tck tck' and I got the answer, didn't I? The same three blokes I had caught earlier walked out. One said, 'We had one net left and some more

Poachers display their rabbits. Before the First World War a poacher who committed a third offence faced a seven-year jail sentence.

pegs and we caught thirteen rabbits.' I said, 'That's unlucky for you, you're not having the rabbits or the nets to go home with.'

Times were hard in the 1930s. Local people had large families and they wanted something to eat and they'd go and get a rabbit. We had a system that we didn't take rabbit poachers to court and we caught many, many, many of those. They had to pay £1 to the nearest hospital or infirmary and get a receipt and send it to the estate office. We used to give them a real good ticking off and say, 'Don't you come again or you know what could happen.' If they worked on the estate there was a very grave risk that they would lose their jobs and their houses. So they made sure they didn't get caught again.

We gamekeepers had as much authority, probably more authority, on the estate than the local policeman. The gamekeeper was always about and had to be very, very observant, so they provided security not just only for the game department but for the whole of the estate.

Margaret Peacock

Margaret Peacock, born in 1915 in Maidwell in Northamptonshire, was heavily influenced by her father's socialist principles. A skilful carpenter and a community-minded man, her father often turned his hand to doing odd jobs in the village for free and he ran the National Deposit Society, which enabled villagers to get medical treatment in return for making regular savings. After several jobs in service, Margaret married in 1939. She has two daughters and lives in Milton Keynes.

The squire would come to the village school on his horse. When there was heavy snow he would come round at playtime and say, 'I want you, you and you to come and sweep a pathway to the pond.' He had a skating party on the lake that evening because the ice was very heavy in those days. My brother said, 'No, Dad said we can't, we're not allowed to.' The squire said, 'I know who your father is, old Bill Deacon.' He laughed then. It didn't bother him. We did feel a bit out of it. Dad said, 'Never mind about that, you're not waiting on him, he can pay people to do it.'

The squire ran the villages and dominated them. He'd come on his horse and people were even scared to ask about repairs to their homes. But my mum and dad paid rent: they weren't in tied property. My father was very strong willed and had got into politics through his parents. He joined the Labour party and went to their meetings. It was great when any election came. It was a big event. They had meetings in the village nearing election time and about a dozen or so men would come down and go on a soapbox and address the village. Everybody was out there, including us children, and the 'Red Flag' would be sung.

Domestic servants at a Devon country house in the 1900s. Keeping a big house running smoothly relied on employing a large number of staff.

Dad told us once that the Conservative candidate was coming to speak. There were posters all over the village. So my brothers, myself and two or three other girls had an idea to sabotage the meeting. In our school lunch hour we went up to the Conservative's car. He'd gone to lunch at the squire's. It was a little car with a funny back that you could sit on. We threw turves of earth in it and filled it up with them. My brother and I wrote slogans all over the car with the school chalk. Then we hared back to school. In stalked the Conservative candidate and demanded to know who had done it, in front of the whole school. My brothers didn't mind owning up. That was it. We all lined up against the wall and the boys were hit with a ruler. Of course, my parents had to be told. Although Dad was very pleased secretly, he had to reprimand us because it was wrong to do such a thing.

In those days there was no other work in the village; the girls went into service and most of the boys went on the farm. My father was doing some work in the Big House and the nanny asked him, as the nursery maid was leaving, whether I would like to replace her. I was fourteen and I passed the interview. My uniform was a checked dress and an apron, which I had to put on at meal times.

I'd go up to my attic room with my candle in a candlestick. There was no electricity or other lights. The candle had to be put out at half past nine and Nanny would come up to see if you were asleep. I wasn't happy because I liked to read and so at night-time I would put my coat along the bottom of the door so the light wouldn't show through, and hide the books under the bed. There was just myself and what we called a scullery maid, the lowest in the kitchen, in the next room, and we used to tap messages on the wall. Was she all right? Was I all right? Just for something to do then. In the mornings I overslept because of reading too late so she would bash and wake me up and that's how we'd go.

A girl learns to ride at Petworth House, Sussex in 1928. Children were introduced to hunting at a young age.

I had to be up at six-thirty to get the fires going in the nursery and get the breakfast for the two small children. I'd have to get them dressed and go down to the dairy in the basement of the house to get the cream for the children's porridge. It was in a jug and I thought, 'Why can't I have some of this? I'm older than them.' So of course I stuck my finger in and helped myself before I got up the stairs. I felt very satisfied doing it.

I missed home because this particular place was so isolated. I used to take the children round and round the grounds – there were enough grounds to build lots of houses on. I met her Ladyship one day and she said something about how the children were and I remarked, 'Very well', smiled and walked off. Two days later the nanny told me off because I didn't say my Ladyship to her when I addressed her and in future would I please say 'my Lady'. Nanny was a tyrant. I don't think she liked me and I didn't like her. I had to help make Nanny's bed as well as the children's and she would leave her clothes on the floor. But I didn't think I was employed to wait on Nanny so I left them, which didn't go in my favour. I was a bit of a rebel in those days. I did everything that I shouldn't do as regards doing my housework. I was supposed to spend ages doing it but instead of that I would give a signal to the footman and he'd come out and we swapped stories and had a good laugh.

I had various jobs like cleaning the prams, which I had to dust and polish their big wheels until they shone. I had to polish the children's shoes. They had pairs for every occasion: red ones to go with red outfits, green ones and lace-ups. It upset me and made me angry. In our village there was still children who couldn't go to school because they hadn't any shoes to put on. I had to look after and pander to these two small children; whatever they wanted more or less had to happen. If they wanted to throw a toy away across the other side of the room they'd say, 'Pick it up! Pick it up!' and I'd have to pick it up and put it back in the big wooden box, and they would do it again, deliberately, to aggravate. I think Nanny may have tried to instil in them that we were lower class and they were upper and that we, as servants, would always have to respect their wishes. We were not allowed to tell them off or protest if they did anything wrong. We could do it through Nanny and, if she felt inclined, she would correct them.

One of the things Nanny instilled in us when she told us what to do and what not to was that I would have to try and lose my village accent. I said, 'What are the words I'm supposed to say?' And she said, 'Well, you say to the children, "Ain't you gonna do this?" You have to say, "Aren't you going to do this?" in a proper manner.' So of course I goes home and repeats what I've been told to mother and the children and, of course, after a few months they all began to think I'm getting very snobby. They started to say, 'Oh, it's rubbing off, you're talking differently.' I think I did lose my accent after a little while.

We were allowed one half-day a week off and every other Sunday if we were lucky. But in the job I had we had to fit in with the children. On this particular half-day I was supposed to have off, Nanny came about two hours before I was due to finish work and said, 'Oh, you can't go today, the children have some visitors'. I must have looked very crestfallen. I said, 'Well my mother will be waiting for me, she is meeting me halfway.' Nanny said, 'Well, it's too bad. She will realise that something has come up.' I just stood there and said, 'Nanny, I want my day off. It was cancelled last time and I'm going.' With that I marched out of the nursery up to my room, got my coat and marched out of the house. I remember standing in the garden feeling really thrilled. I thought I'd got one over somebody and it satisfied me as regards rebelling against the system, shall we say. Of course, I didn't think of the consequences.

The next day Dad was mending antique furniture for his Lordship and he said, 'What have you been up to?' He said Nanny had just come and told him that I couldn't stop in the job because she didn't think I was satisfactory and she was very sorry but I had to go at the end of the month. I expected Dad to be really annoyed but he laughed and said, 'Well, you shouldn't do that, you should do what you're told. It's your first job and you won't get a reference.'

I was so relieved to think that I had not got to obey the rules and regulations of the household any more and I vowed in my mind I would never work in a big house like that where there were so many restrictions and 'do's' and 'don'ts' and bows and curtseys. I was really thrilled to be out.

– Three –

The Price of Innocence

In the summer of 1914, the villagers of Morchard Bishop in South Devon drove out from their parish an unmarried couple who were 'living in sin'. The post office where they lived was splattered with an ox bladder full of blood, then the village band paraded around with effigies of the couple before ritually burning them behind the chapel. The victims fled to Exeter, never to return. This was known in the West Country as a 'skimmity ride', a not uncommon way of showing village disapproval for those who defied sexual convention. In rural Lincolnshire and Cambridgeshire similar incidents were recorded between the wars. There it was known as 'ran tan tan' or 'rough music'. Villagers would bang

This girl and boy look the picture of innocence but for some youngsters the privacy of country lanes and fields provided too much sexual temptation.

together pots and pans, calling out the names of the offenders, who were often forced to leave the area. The custom graphically illustrates the sexual mores in the countryside during the first decades of the century and the retribution meted out by village communities to those who broke their taboos.

The Church was a major influence on attitudes towards courtship, sex and marriage in the countryside. It wielded enormous power before the last war, especially in villages where it was often the focus of social life and the mainspring of

public morality. Parish priests continued to preach the sanctity of marriage and the sin of 'fornication'. So, too, did the non-conformist preachers who were so influential in many thousands of villages throughout Britain from the north-east coast of Scotland (the stronghold of millennial evangelism) down to Cornwall where primitive Methodism was a force to be reckoned with. There was also strong disapproval of sex outside marriage from a host of organizations active in villages such as the Boy Scouts, the Band of Hope and the Social Purity Movement.

The concern to promote sexual abstinence before marriage was largely inspired by the Victorian values that were particularly deep-rooted in rural Britain. It was also partly a response to the practical dangers of sex during this era. Contraception was far less safe than today, heightening the danger of unwanted pregnancies. And venereal disease was a major health problem for which there was no cure. In the 1920s deaths from syphilis reached 60,000 a year. Most of these deaths were concentrated in the towns and cities where prostitution thrived, and country people were keen to maintain the good health that often seemed to be the reward for moral purity.

Sex was a taboo subject for children growing up in the countryside before the last war. Like their urban counterparts, the vast majority remained ignorant of the facts of life well into their teens. On farms, in villages and even in the Big House there seems to have been a conspiracy of silence among parents. As a result, the onset of puberty could be traumatic, especially for girls. Many had no idea what was happening when their periods started: some thought they were dying or that it was a punishment from God. Children learned what little they knew about sex by observing animals and through sexual play in the secluded fields and woods. Their sexual ignorance was reinforced by the absence of any formal sex education in all schools – an attitude which received widespread parental support. When in 1913, a feminist schoolmistress in the Derbyshire village of Dronfield gave her class sex instruction, the children's disgusted parents signed a 1,200-strong petition demanding her resignation. The mothers felt that teaching their young children about sex was an affront to their moral innocence and would stir a prurient interest in sex.

Children were utterly unprepared for the sexual harassment that some would have to face in the adult world of work on the land or in the Big House. Most began work at the age of thirteen or fourteen, and the girls hired as servants on lonely hill farms often found they were the only female apart from the farmer's wife for miles around. They could become the target for unwanted sexual advances and harassment from the farmer and his labourers. To protect themselves they relied on instinct. Marian Atkinson, now ninety-four, worked as a servant on hill farms in the Lake District while in her teens between 1918 and 1922:

Opposite
A spinster is rewarded with a crown for keeping her virginity until her death, in a Hampshire village ceremony. The gloves symbolized gauntlets which challenged any man to refute the claim within three weeks.

'I went to a farm when I was fifteen and I had no interest in boys at that age. And this horseman started following me round and round the barn. He would put his hand up me frock or nip me at the back of my knees. Of course you bashed their hands down. But this particular time he was sitting in the barn and he unbuttoned his trousers and showed me what he had, showed me his penis. And he said, "Do you know what this is for Marian?" Of course, as daft as swill I was, I said, "Yes, to pee out of." Didn't know no different. He said, "If you come over here I'll show you." Of course, I began to get 'feard [afraid] then and thought there's more in this than meets the eye. And I turned tail and ran.'

Youngsters working on a Scottish farm. Sex was such a taboo among country children that girls were often ordered indoors when the stallion served the mare.

Village boys and girls had a very restricted choice of sweethearts. Many courted those they had known at school. The boys in many villages assumed that local girls were theirs to have and to hold. They would fight off any outsiders who infringed what they regarded as their territorial rights. Even a boy from a neighbouring village might be seen as a threatening interloper to be driven away if he so much as tried his luck with a village girl. Fred Wigby, who grew up in the Norfolk village of Wicklewood, discovered the strength of feeling that surrounded this unwritten code of conduct when he went on his first date at the age of fourteen in 1927:

'Oh dear, I met this girl as I was keeping cows by the side of the road. She was a servant. You were not supposed to go into another village for a girl. Nobody dared go to Wymondham. You had a Wicklewood girl or you had a Wicklewood girl.

My sister said, "Where are you a going?"

I said, "I'm a going courting."

"If you're going courting you've got to clean your teeth." I was on the floor in three seconds and she put the brush up the kitchen chimney and cleaned my teeth with soot. Then I cycled to Wymondham on my new bike and met the girl. There were a lot of boys about and the ginger-haired ringleader shouted, "Go home, foreigner!" But I felt so big with my new cycle, I stood my ground. The next thing I knew my cycle was grabbed and they threw me over the blackthorn hedge. A brand new bike – and me – straight over! As I got up I saw she was walking away with the ginger one that did it. I never went out with a girl for years after that. Once was enough!'

The introduction between the two world wars of regular motor-bus services linking outlying villages with each other and with nearby market towns, played a vital role in extending the choice of partners in country areas. A new pattern of courtship began to emerge in which boys and girls met partners from further afield at the cinema, the dance hall, or promenading up and down the main street on the market town 'monkey run'. The young conductors on the village bus routes could themselves benefit from this opening up of romantic opportunities. Florence Bowley, born in 1910, grew up in Crays Hill, a small Essex village which became a regular stop for the new motor-bus route from London to Southend in the 1920s:

'I was a thoroughly modern young woman with my Eton crop and flannel trousers. Some of the women in the village disapproved of me and said things like, "She looks like a boy", but I told them, "I do what I like". I plucked my eyebrows, I wore cream powder and lipstick, which was very unusual in the villages in those days, and I smoked. I just wanted to have fun and when the buses started coming through the village that was great. They were single-deckers, chocolate-coloured New Empress Saloons. Our village was a stop-off point and I got a job as a waitress providing the crews and the passengers with refreshments.

'Of course, I got to know all the conductors – I thought they were very attractive in their smart uniforms. I had romances with quite a few of them. I knew the timetable back to front and when the last bus went past I would have a candle

Country buses allowed people to court further afield. This 1932 service took men from the Forest of Dean to their sweethearts most of whom worked as servants in Cheltenham.

burning in my window to show I was awake. One of them, a chap called Leslie, he would stop the bus and drop off a box of chocolates. I'd nip out and we'd have a kiss over the gate. After a time they'd let me travel for free on the buses and if it was empty I'd often be on the back seat with the conductor going to Southend and back again. It was great fun.'

Many country couples dared not risk sex before marriage. The young woman was expected to be a virgin bride and courtship involved the observance of a ritual of female innocence and chastity. This ritual was especially important to the daughters of the aristocracy and gentry. Making a good marriage was one of their main aims in life and virginity was a prized asset in this market. To ensure that it was not lost, their social movements were closely supervised by mothers, governesses and chaperones until they were in their late teens or early twenties.

Sexual self-restraint for all classes in the countryside was made more difficult by the lengthy period of engagement and high age of marriage in the first decades of the century. During the Edwardian era the average age of marriage was higher than it had ever been in British history, peaking at twenty-seven years for men and twenty-six for women. In rural areas the sons of farmers were often financially dependent on their parents and some postponed marriage until they took over or inherited the family farm. Courting couples were under great pressure and many succumbed to the temptation of sex before marriage. With little knowledge of birth control and virtually no way of obtaining contraceptives in the villages, they were taking a great risk. Illicit sex was surrounded by guilt and fear. The experience of Gwen Taylor, brought up in the village of Kempshot near Basingstoke was fairly typical. In 1936, at the age of seventeen, she made love for the first time with her fiancé after a walk down a country lane.

'I took a lot of persuading, because it was my upbringing, but he'd already asked me to marry him and get engaged, so I thought, "Oh well, he'll wonder why I'm stalling," so that was it. But it was very difficult going home that night. It was awkward because my father always looked you up and down very closely when you walked in the house to see if you looked guilty. And I had a job not looking guilty.'

If the young woman got pregnant a wedding was invariably hastily arranged to avoid any scandal. The few British sex surveys covering the first half of the century suggest that as many as half of all those who risked sex before marriage got pregnant. Such was the fear of the stigma of illegitimacy, a few married hastily on the basis of imagined and mistaken pregnancies. Ernie Gray, born in 1913, began courting a local girl in the Cambridgeshire Fens at the age of twenty-one.

'She was only fifteen and we went out for a year. Well you was always alone in the Fens, it was a lonely place, there wasn't a house within half a mile. We was

Fashion-conscious Florence Bowley found romance on the buses in the 1920s.

kissing and cuddling all the time and then something else cropped up. If you wanted to have connections you could bop down anywhere, no problem. Nobody else to see; there was only your two selves there. And that's what we did. We had a lovely life there, we really began to enjoy ourselves. Of course there was no protection, I didn't know of anything like that.

   'She was sixteen now and one day her mother came up to me and said I would have to marry her because she was expecting a baby. I said, "I'll marry her, I love

Sweet nothings whispered over a country gate were often as far as lovers like these in the early 1900s dared to go.

her very much and I like you too, you're a lovely mother." And we got married just a few weeks later. But the strange thing was, she wasn't pregnant and she never had the baby. I've often puzzled about that because we never had children. Anyway, I had sixty-three years with her and when I lost her three years ago we'd had the happiest years that anybody could have.'

An old North-umbrian custom observed at a Holy Island wedding in 1936. After the couple jump over a stone in the churchyard, fishermen fire a shotgun to bring luck.

The disreputable 'shotgun wedding' was extremely common in the first decades of the century in both country and city. But there were many women whose lovers refused to stand by them, usually disclaiming it was their baby and fleeing the area. Every year in the 1920s and 1930s, there were around 25,000–35,000 pregnancies among unmarried women. Illegitimacy in Britain was generally higher in the countryside than in the cities. Some counties, such as the North Riding of Yorkshire, Herefordshire and rural Nottinghamshire, were in the top ten for illegitimacy rates from the mid-nineteenth to the mid-twentieth centuries. And in Scotland the north-eastern county of Banffshire consistently had the highest illegitimacy rate in the country from the 1850s to the 1930s.

The unmarried mother had to face the stigma of illegitimacy. It was possibly greater in the countryside than in the city because of the closely-knit nature of village communities. There was no escape from the gossip and the blame, which was generally directed towards the 'fallen woman'. The more fortunate were looked after by their parents and went back to work to help support the baby. But many were driven from their homes, lost their jobs and had to seek refuge in the parish workhouse. Others found sanctuary in mother and baby homes in nearby towns and cities, run by organizations like the Salvation Army. Invariably their baby would be adopted, sometimes against their will. The most unfortunate ended up in mental hospitals, of which there was no shortage in the countryside. Countless thousands were locked away under the Mental Defectives Act of 1913, which defined them as feeble-minded and detained them indefinitely. Some never got out and their child was also brought up in the institution as a mental defective.

The country couples who played it safe and refrained from sex before marriage could have their own problems too. The romantic climax of the wedding night was sometimes a disaster as neither partner knew what to do. The widespread extent of non-consummated marriages was documented in the thousands of letters written to birth-control campaigner Marie Stopes in the 1920s and 1930s. In these cases, the woman had such profound associations between sex and sin it took some time before she could begin a sexual relationship with her husband. Smiler Marshall married his sweetheart Florence in the village of Elmstead Market in 1924, after five years' service in the Essex Yeomanry during the First World War.

'I knew a bit myself because during the war I had a great do with this Belgian woman – cor she was smashing! I reckon I was with her for three weeks and I done her every day – smashing! Well, you learn something see. But my wife wasn't interested in anything like that for months after we married. Because when we were courting her mother had told her that if I ever suggested anything naughty to her, she wasn't to go out with me any more.

'Her mother had frightened her. I lost some sweat over that. Never mind, at the finish we had three children and twins. We had a wonderful marriage together. And now I've got two sons alive, twelve grandchildren, twenty-two great grandchildren and five great, great grandchildren.'

The taboos on sex meant that many of the pregnancies of married mothers were unplanned or unwanted. Birth control was, even for married couples living in rural areas, as late as the 1930s, often not available and certainly not respectable. Most country doctors refused or did not know how to give contraceptive advice: it was seen as immoral and threatening to the mother's 'natural' reproductive role. Many poorer families could not afford the doctor anyway. Although the first birth-control clinics for women, inspired by Marie Stopes, began during the inter-war years, there were still only a dozen in the early 1930s, all of which concentrated their work in the towns and cities. In rural areas contraception was normally left to the husband but condoms or 'French letters' were rarely stocked in village shops and most men were too embarrassed to ask for them. Instead, they used the unreliable method of withdrawal. As a result many pregnancies were unplanned or unwanted.

A young man claims his kiss – or a forfeit – from the village girls on the annual 'Tutti' day in Hungerford, Berkshire.

Ignorance about contraception was matched by a lack of knowledge among mothers-to-be about childbirth itself. In the first decades of the century many countrywomen having their first baby had little or no idea what to expect. In many villages pregnancy and childbirth were almost as taboo as the sex act itself as subjects for information and conversation. Some went into labour believing that the baby would come out of their umbilicus or even their anus. The pain of childbirth was made worse by ignorance and fear.

Childbirth was especially dangerous for mothers in country areas, partly due to the shortage of trained midwives and nurses. As late as 1925, almost 20 per cent of the population of West Suffolk had no district nurse available to them. Mothers made do with the services of the village handywoman whose other jobs included laying out the dead. As a consequence of the shortage of medical facilities in the countryside the maternal mortality rate was higher in many rural areas than it was in the cities.

Pregnancy and childbirth dominated many married women's lives during the first decades of the century. In the 1900s, rural working-class women experienced an average of ten pregnancies. Of these around three would end in miscarriage and two in death during birth or infancy. They could expect to spend around fifteen years either pregnant or nursing babies. Rural middle-class women generally had fewer children, on average about three in the 1900s. There was a gradual reduction in the birth rate and family size throughout Britain between the 1900s and the 1930s which continued after the Second World War. This was due to greater awareness of birth control and a determined effort to improve living standards by having fewer children and, if necessary, abstaining from sex to achieve this. But this trend was much slower to take effect in the countryside. Here large families with four, five, six or more children remained commonplace. There remained a significant minority of rural families with eight, nine, ten or more children. Albert Gillett, born in the Cambridgeshire Fens in 1923, was the father of nine children.

'There are lots of jokes about living in the country and having a large family. They say it's because we didn't have electricity or anything else to do of an evening and we went to bed early. I don't know whether that's true, but I certainly was highly sexed. I never do anything by halves. I was brought up a strict Methodist and sexual intercourse was definitely not for me until I was married, but I made up for it from then onwards. I became a Methodist lay preacher in the village and I think it was my religion that made me feel strongly that any birth control was wrong. I never used it. I believed, and still do, that sex is for procreation and you accept the children that come as God's gift and He will help you provide for them. That's what happened to me.

'When we started having babies I desperately wanted a girl. The first four were sons but the fifth was a daughter. Then we had another daughter, then another daughter and, lo and behold, another daughter and the last was a boy, so we were wonderfully blessed with all these children. We worked hard to care for them and I went on to run the village shop so I could get lots of things cheap for us. That helped. We were very happy, I have no regrets at all.'

Most often the women having these very large families were the wives of agricultural labourers or small tenant farmers. The burden on them was enormous as they were expected to work in the fields as well as bring up the children. Yet most women accepted these circumstances as the inevitable consequence of being a wife and mother.

Raymond Crees

Raymond Crees spent the 1930s working as a footman and then a butler in the large country houses. He left in 1940 to join the armed forces.

When we sat down to eat, the maids would sit on one side of the table and all the men servants on the other and it would occur to me, 'Why not rub ankles with these pretty country girls under the table?' But you didn't dare do that because down at the end of the table sat the head housemaid – an ogress – and she wasn't going to have any of her girls sullied by you touching them under the table. You had to wait for other opportunities.

I fell deeply in love with one of the housemaids in the Big House and we had to have clandestine meetings. Her half-day was different to mine but love will always find a way and so we worked out a plan. On my half-day I would go to the cinema and when I came back I used to wait until the house was quiet, about ten o'clock, and go around under her window and throw some gravel up off the drive. Then the light would come on and she would come downstairs and let me in.

There were plenty of places where one could go in the garden which were hardly ever used. We would go down in the moonlight to the lake, strip off and swim. It was paradise. We would meet out in the grounds, go for a walk and get lost in the woods around the back of the Big House, lay down in the leaves, make daisy chains and make love. If I'd been out with my lady friend in the bushes, of course, I would come back a little bit dishevelled and dirty. The pressing room was near the back door, nowhere near the butler's pantry, so I was safe. I would nip in there, strip off and press my trousers. I would brush my clothes and polish my silver buttons and my livery, and present myself at table as immaculate as always and do my duty in the dining room.

We enjoyed ourselves whenever we could. Of course had we ever been caught we would have been instantly dismissed. I wouldn't have got a reference and without a reference in private service in those days one couldn't get a job. It was one big risk. One just had to take terrible chances because it was the rather nicer part of life that made up for some of the grim aspects of life in the Big Houses in those days.

If my girl was one of the maids cleaning the footmen's rooms, including mine, I'd arrange to meet her in my room. I had to change into my livery at about eleven o'clock every morning. I knew we would be safe for at least half an hour. The bed was unmade and invitingly open. She'd got a glitter in her eye and we made love in the bed. It was one way of having sex when it was winter and damn cold outside.

We had sex in the house whenever we could. There was one charming occasion when I caught her in the Ladyship's bedroom. I had to go in there to pick up a tray and the bed was wide open and ready. We got in there and thoroughly enjoyed ourselves. One sexually reaches a certain point when one couldn't care less of the consequences. You've just got to follow it through to the end. And, of course, it was always exciting to taste 'forbidden fruit' and have sexual relations. It gave one an extra buzz to think that you might be caught. It was like Russian roulette, really.

Another time I was sitting in the servant's hall and there was no one else there. My girlfriend came in and just removed an article of clothing and sat on my lap. We had a lovely time and it seemed to go on forever. Then in the midst of it the head housemaid came in to give some instructions to my girlfriend. It was bad enough to catch her sitting on my lap but she couldn't get up while the housemaid was in the room otherwise I should have been in a terrible state. Consequently the girl had to sit tight to me until the housemaid had finished giving her instructions and left the servants' hall.

Lovers on the Isle of Man in 1939. Every year in the 1920s and 1930s there were up to 35,000 pregnancies among unmarried women, many in rural Britain.

Secret romances in service were common: servants in isolated country houses had little chance to meet people outside their own limited world.

All the footmen knew that I was having a sexual relationship with the girls the same as they were having with their own hand-picked girls. So no one told on anyone else because we were all in it together. I'm sure the gentry just hadn't the foggiest idea of what was going on sometimes in the Big Houses. They only knew that when they rang a bell a servant would appear and serve them with whatever they wanted. I don't think they thought much about what went on behind the green baize door.

Not that they were innocents. One summer country house, where I was a footman, had been very busy all through the season. These people had a house in Eaton

Square in London with its own staff, and staff in a big house in Scotland for the grouse shooting. Her Ladyship said that she and his Lordship would be going up to Eaton Square and we staff would have a rest. She told me that the Honourable Mr Edward was staying in residence but she had told him he was not allowed to have anyone else in the House and there was to be no entertaining. Well, hardly had the slinky tyres left the drive than he was on the phone to his cousin in London. It was a very primitive telephone system and, of course, being a good servant I listened in – one had to know what was going on. He said, 'Oh Monty, bring a couple of girls from the Windmill Theatre down for the weekend and we'll have a whale of a time.'

So of course I told the staff and the staff went on strike in a manner of speaking. The cook said, 'If they think they're going to have an eight-course dinner then they're not, they can only have six. I'll punish them.' The head house-maid said the two girls would be going to the Peacock room, which was a four-poster bedroom at the end of a corridor which was so dim and gloomy I called it the haunted chamber. We always used to put the guests who never gave us a tip in there to get our own back. That night at about midnight I looked across the Great Hall and under the drawing room door there was a light and I could hear music being played on a gramophone. I presumed the four people were all in there dancing. I took the guest's cases upstairs and I never bothered to knock. As I went in there were these two couples on the four-poster bed and it was rocking to and fro like a ship on the Bay of Biscay.

The next morning Mr Monty called me into his room and said, 'Did you see anything last night, John?' So I said in a hesitating manner, 'Well. . .' and he said, 'Pass me my wallet.' And so I passed him his wallet and he gave me a huge £5 note. When I went to call Mr Edward he said, 'Did you see anything last night, John?' I said, 'Well. . .'. I collected £10 that morning and my salary was only £14 so I had a good view the night before and £10 to boot!

That was just one of the sexual activities that went on in the Big House. Of course, the gentry would play something called sardines, it's an old Edwardian game, a sort of hide-and-seek. People weren't found for hours and hours but it was quite fun because, of course, we knew where they were hiding and we used to purposely discover them as we went about our work.

Mary Rowling

Mary Rowling, now seventy-eight, worked as a servant girl on the Cumbrian hill farms. Her own brothers had treated her as a 'skivvy' on her father's farm so she was well-prepared for the chauvinism of the farming world in the 1930s.

A teenage Mary Rowling in her native Cumbria.

Opposite Haymaking was an exhausting but enjoyable communal activity – and often a good way of striking up a romance.

Some of the farmers were randy, and some of the farm men too. They were a bit too near nature, living on the farms, weren't they? I had to fight a few of them off. They were the worst when their wives were pregnant and they were trying to use you as a stand-in.

Loads of the girls had a baby. Nearly every time I met up with friends for a night out they'd say, 'So-and-so is expecting. She's got herself into a lot of trouble with the farmer or one of the farm men.' You were conscious of it all the time. There were no way of getting any money out of him, nobody would have believed the girl in a court of law. They'd say, 'Oh, she has her nights out, we never know what she's up to.' They'd just take the farmer's word against a servant girl's. You had no one to turn to. The police would have laughed you out of the place if you had said, 'One of the farmers has been trying to grope me.' If you got raped you wouldn't have dared tell anybody. They would just call you a silly beggar for not looking after yourself.

So you'd have to be very careful. You got the signals clear enough; when they were passing you in a passage or meeting you with a couple of buckets, they managed to put their hands on you where they shouldn't. 'Watch it!' I'd say. 'Plenty of room. Get past.' You'd have to keep them at arm's length and use your brains – and your iron-clogged toes if necessary. It made 'em coil back very quickly if you were a good shin boner! Sometimes they'd try and sweet-talk you a bit. 'Have you seen how the calves are getting on? Have you seen how well the little 'un's getting on? Just have a look.' I'd say, 'I'll have a look up when I go and feed it.' I thought, 'You're not enticing me into no cowshed on me own.'

This one farmer, he were a bit on the sweet-talking side. I'd gone into the cowshed at night to get the hay down for the morning as usual and he'd been watching me. The farmer's wife was indoors with the children, getting ready for bed, and I thought, 'Well, I'll keep hold of me pitchfork, I won't leave go,' as he was lurking about. I'd nearly finished and then I'd caught the rustle of the hay. I thought, 'Hey up, he's going to jump across to where I am and cut me off by the ladder.' He started coming over. 'What do you want?' I said.

'I'm just coming up, like, for a little cuddle, you know.'

I says, 'Back down there. I will, I'll stick this pitchfork through yer belly. I won't think twice.'

'He says, 'Nay, you wouldn't do that to the boss, would you?' He were crawling a bit nearer. So I set off towards him with the fork ready and he backed off just in time. I thought I'd kill his courage one way or another.

I said, 'I shall tell your wife when I get downstairs what you've been up to.' And I did. She asked me not to go and said she couldn't give me my money as he kept it. I'd been there five months of my six-month hiring but as I broke it I didn't get anything. But he got nowt neither! And at the hirings where I knew he'd be looking for a new servant girl, I made sure that I passed the word around that he was a randy old git.

Ruth Armstrong

Born in 1906, Ruth Armstrong still lives in rural Wiltshire where she grew up and, like many village girls of her generation, fell in love with 'the boy next door'. Ruth and her farm labourer husband married in 1925 and had seven girls and one boy at a time when many rural mothers had to cope with primitive conditions such as no electricity and no running water. For Ruth life was doubly hard: she was handicapped in one leg after contracting polio when she was six.

Ruth Armstrong as a young woman in Wiltshire.

It was on a Sunday afternoon when I was seventeen. There was a great do on in the village because the memorial was being unveiled for the First World War. All of a sudden I had a terrible headache and I couldn't think why because I had a pig Panama hat on. When I woke up at home the next morning I saw blood on the sheet. I screamed to my mother that I was bleeding and she came running in the door. 'Shut up! Shut up! Your brother will hear. Don't let your brother hear. Shut the door.' So I said, 'What is it? I haven't cut myself.' She said, 'I've got something to tell you. You're a girl and every month you will have this happen.' She got some things and showed me how to put them on. Oh, I was really frightened and she wanted me to go to the shop to get something. I wouldn't go, I thought Mr Cave would know I had it on me. I thought it was terrible. I remember saying to her, 'Does the Queen have it?' She said, 'Oh yes, all ladies, all women.'

I knew nothing of sex. We didn't use the word. I'd known the boy I was to marry since I was thirteen. He told me later he fell in love with me then. We all started going around together with his brother and two more young lads and three of us girls out on the Downs. They used to throw us in the corn and shoot the grasses at us and we used to steal their handkerchiefs. We were all innocent and that's how I liked it.

When I was about eighteen he asked me for a date one Sunday night. He was five years older than me. We went over the hill and sat on the gate in the moonlight and talked about a lot of different things. He said, 'Will you go out with me forever?' I said, 'Oh, we'll see.' I went to get off the gate and he put his arms around me to kiss me and I smacked him in the face. I said, 'People only kiss when they're engaged.' And he said, 'I'll get engaged to you when I've got enough money to buy a ring.' And it started from there. I started to love him quite a lot. He was like a big brother and a lover as well.

After he asked me to marry him, my mother took him to one side and had a good talk to him. 'You must remember Ruth is a cripple but she is a good worker and she is a beautiful cook,' she said. Well, being as he lived next door he said, 'I can see what Ruth can do. I'm not worried. I'm marrying her because I love her.'

One night we were sitting behind a hayrick and he put his arms around me as usual. Then he started rubbing me leg, so I drew away and then he started to put his hand up my clothes. I said, 'Don't you do that to me.'

He said, 'Well we're getting married soon, aren't we?'

I said, 'Yes, 'course we are.'

'Well,' he said, 'you'll know what to expect.'

I said, 'I don't want to know.'

On our wedding night I blew the candle out before I took my clothes off. I didn't like a man to see me undressed even if it was my sweetheart. He said to me, 'Well, you're going to get in bed with me, aren't you?' I said yes. He said, 'Well, what did you put the candle out for to take your clothes off?' I done that for two or three nights. It was frightening at first but then, of course, it began to get loving and natural. I never saw my husband naked in my life, never. He always had these pyjamas on.

When I was first pregnant I went up to my mother and said, 'Something's wrong with me.' I didn't know what it was and she asked me for some details and said, 'You know what that is, don't you? You're going to have a baby.' I said, 'Oh, where's it going to come from?' She said, 'You'll find out.' So I went down and asked my husband and he said he had no idea.

When I went into labour I had a very bad stomach ache and I thought it was the rhubarb I'd had for my dinner. But it began to get worse. I was in such pain that I tore the lace curtains down from the window. I caught hold of them and pulled on them because I was in such pain I didn't know what to do. My husband went to get the doctor and midwife. I got all dolled up in bed with me new sheets and me lacey night-dress ready to have the baby. I bought them to have the baby in. I had this all on.

The midwife came in and said, 'You will have to take all that off.' I understood afterwards why. It was a terrible thing having a baby. All you had for the pain was a bath towel tied on the back of the iron bedstead and you pulled on that. I said to the midwife, 'Where's it going to come out from?' 'From the same place as it went in.' I didn't know what she meant. I thought it came from your belly button and it would stretch open and a baby could come from there. I had an awful surprise. It was terrible pain, terrible. I thought I was going to die. I had my little girl at half-past six in the morning.

I went on to have seven more babies. We knew nothing of birth control. We were about nine miles away from the chemist in those days and there was no clinics or anything like that in the village. By the time the village got one I had almost finished my family. The village nurse was the woman who used to lay people out and bring babies in the world and

Not all villages had a district nurse like this one visiting a mother in Sussex in 1930. Pregnant women often relied on the aid of the local 'handywoman'.

ring the church bell. She never told us a thing. I said to her once, 'I love babies but I would rather not have any more.' She said, 'Well, the only thing you can do is tell your husband to withdraw.' Well, he did. Didn't make no blooming difference, though.

When we were expecting, only our own husbands knew. That was private business. We didn't flounce it around for everyone to see. People would gossip, 'Oh, have you heard that Mrs So-and-so is expecting again?'

'How do you know?'

'I saw her the other day and I could tell by her eyes.'

So in my young days we used to wear corsets and pull them in very, very tight. I remember standing at the gate one day and holding one of my little girls in my arms, and the next-door neighbour said, 'Oh, your little girl's getting quite big now isn't she?'

I said, 'Yes, she is.'

She said, 'You don't want any more do you?'

I said, 'Well, if they come along they will.' The second day after, I gave birth and she didn't even know it.

The old women in the village used to say that if you were expecting, to get a pint of beer and warm it and put some soda in and drink it. Or to get ivy leaves from a hedge, boil that and drink it and then you wouldn't have a baby. I thought I'd try it because I was a month gone and I got my husband to get some beer. He was a bit disgusted about it. I warmed the beer and put a lump of soda in it. Oh, my goodness, one sip and I'm glad I was near the sink. It was terrible. I didn't want any more children but I loved them all when they came. I'm glad I had them.

Reg Dobson

Reg Dobson was born in 1913 and grew up on his father's farm at Market Drayton. Reg never had any doubts about being a farmer himself and left the boarding school he hated in Newport to work on the farm when he was fourteen. In 1936 he married and had three children. From the 1950s he farmed in Warwickshire, where he still lives.

Of course, when you're seventeen, there's only two things on your mind: work (Father made sure there was no getting away from that) and sex. I mean, you saw it go on all over the farm, what with the rams and bulls and pigs and that sort of thing. But sex was taboo; my father never told me anything.

You tried to make love to the girls on the farm but most would not wear you at any ruddy price. One of the girls was a bit of a beggar for tormenting us boys. She used to go across the yard in a long skirt down to her damned ankles, lifting it up and saying, 'Come on, catch me.' There was a lad who worked with me who was was about two years older than me and he said, 'Come on, we'll have her.' So we ran after her and caught her in the shed where there was a great big barrel of treacle. We used to put the treacle on the corn for the cows because they loved it. Well, we got this girl, lifted her and put her into this tub. She couldn't get out, of course, so we lifted her out. We had to help her across the yard and she could barely hobble with all the treacle on her. She daren't go in the farmhouse so she went into the cheese room, stripped off and then shot up the back stairs so we couldn't see her undressed. She never tormented us again after that.

My first girl-friend, Freda, was getting on for thirty. I was seventeen. She was one of the maids living in. One night we ran out of water and I had to go to the well. Freda said, 'Oh, I'll come

A fresh-faced Scottish milkmaid: girls on isolated farms where men dominated could often be the only unmarried female for miles around.

with you to fetch it.' We were carrying these buckets of water and we put 'em down. The next thing we were making love. I think she got caught hold of me before I caught hold of her, but that's how it first started. This went on every blinkin' night and every morning. It was a secret. We used to go to bed early, before the others, and make love on the landing. I used to get up at five o'clock and take a cup of tea to her in the morning, get into bed with her and make love to her. Father was sleeping in the bedroom underneath hers. I don't know whether he heard but he never said nothing to me.

Well, I thought it was marvellous in those days. It's calf love, isn't it, when you're seventeen? At seventeen all I thought about was sex more than anything else. We'd got no money to do anything and that was the only bit of fun we had, the girls and boys. It went on for twelve months until I got her in the family way and then that was it. Of course, I was worried to death. My neighbour told Father and he said, 'Oh, the young green horn' (but it wasn't long after that before Father got a woman pregnant with twins and he paid her £500). I was very upset when it came out. Oh Lord, Freda was told to leave, she wasn't asked to leave. I didn't actually have to go to court in person. My neighbour went and said he'd seen her making love to this boy-friend of hers in the fields. Of course the judge didn't take a damned bit of notice of that. He knew Father had got some money and that was it. I had to pay 5s a week. I was getting 10s a week off of father for about eighteen hours a ruddy day and had to buy me own clothes out of that. Father said, 'I'd better give you 15s now.' So he paid for it really.

I had to pay for sixteen years. I would have liked to see my child but you weren't allowed to do that sort of thing. If Father had found out he would have gone mad. That sort of thing happened all over the country, all the while, but as soon as ever the girl got pregnant – out she went. It was not a disgrace to me; it was a disgrace to her. No one thought anything about the men doing it. It was always the poor girl as got sent away. I felt very sorry for her, although she wasn't an innocent girl.

Marian Atkinson

Marian Atkinson gave birth to fifteen healthy children, without gas or anaesthetic, at a time when many babies and mothers died in childbirth. She first met her husband Bill on a school outing when she was twelve and he was thirteen. They met up again a few years later on a farm where she was a servant and he was a labourer. They married in 1924. Marian has fifty grandchildren, eighty-two great grandchildren and five great great grandchildren.

We all sat on a fender in front of the fire and mother sat on a rocking chair, explaining the facts of life to us. She explained through the animals, because living in the country we knew about these things, but she used to say, 'A man and a woman doesn't get together until they get to the marriage bed and that is the first time that your husband sees you naked.' She warned us many, many times about keeping oneself pure and only having one man in your life. I can put my hand on my heart and say I never had sex 'til I was married.

Nine of Marian Atkinson's fifteen-strong brood.

I did not want a great large family; it was just a case, as my mother said, of what God sends you've got to put up with. I knew nothing whatsoever about birth control and neither did my husband. Didn't even know there was such a thing in this world. I can honestly say right through to my last child, my fifteenth, nobody ever mentioned birth control to me in any shape or form. I suppose we would have limited the children if we had known. My husband said, 'We don't want no more kids, I'll withdraw,' but he were never early enough! Looking back on me life I think I was sexually ignorant.

When we had only the one child or two children we were really looking forward to life and what we were going to do for them. One was going to be Prime Minister at one time! But of course they kept coming along and they got nothing. When children come as quick as they came to me it got a burden at times and I used to feel I couldn't put up with any more. When I found that I was pregnant again I used to say to my husband, 'Oh God, not again. How ever are we going to manage?' When I found that I was pregnant, probably the ninth or tenth time, and I told my husband about it, he said, 'It's all your fault.' We really got into an argument. That night I forsaked his bed and went to sleep with the girls – that was his punishment – probably for a week. But we never went to bed on a row. I always said, 'Good night Bill, I'm going to bed now,' and I'd get up next morning and would say, 'Your breakfast is ready.'

My husband and I never discussed sex or anything alluding to it in any shape or form in front of the children. Anything we had to say to each other we said behind the bedroom door. The many times I did have to tell him that I was pregnant I always told him quietly when none of the children were in hearing.

Sometimes I was still working on the farm we managed, right up until the hour the baby was born. When the pains got so bad you was sort of bending over yourself and gasping for breath and saying, 'Oh, I'll have to give in now, I'll have to go and get on the bed and wait for the eventful birth.' The next day it was back to me labours and looking after me kids because I couldn't afford to be in bed and the children had to be looked after.

Before my sixth child was born I was decorating a prize-winning Jersey cow for a show the next day in Cartmel. I had to clean it, wash it, scrape its hooves, and comb its hair and tail. My husband was there with me and I said, 'I'm going to have the baby today.'

He said, 'What do you mean? It's not due yet.'

I said, 'I've had a bit of a grind in me back. You had better go and find the district nurse. I'll be all right on my own.' Well, my eldest daughter at that time was twelve years old and she was capable of looking after the younger ones so I went upstairs and laid on the bed.

My husband come tearing back on his bike – couldn't find the district nurse because she'd gone to church – but he'd left a message. When she arrived me baby was on the bed. 'Course, I hadn't been able to cut the cord so it was still attached to the afterbirth, laid alongside me on the bed. She did what had to be done and made me a cup of tea.

I had an old woman for the first five who had no qualifications whatsoever, she just did it for a living, and charged 7s for the fortnight. The old handywoman never used to mince her words. She used to put a rolled towel around the bed head and she used to say, 'Hang on to it and pull, lass, shout if you want, scream out if you want it. Don't make no difference to me, I'm doing my job, you do yours.' But as time went on we got a district nurse and she lived six miles away. If you had a doctor in childbirth you had to pay two guineas – that's why I never had one in.

I had thirteen children when I was on the farm and I always had a toddler and a baby in arms and a baby expected. I got up at about half past five every morning and got the cows in from the field and fed them and milked all seventeen on a three-legged stool before I dashed back in the house to get all the kids up and give them breakfast: flapjacks which were fried like pancakes on a griddle pan.

As soon as I'd seen the children off to school and given the younger ones their breakfast, washed and dressed them, then I had to let me cows out, clean the cow shed with a barrow and a brush, go outside across to the pigsty where I had to feed fifty pigs, and pick up fifty buckets of water from a well and empty these into troughs. I had to take the children that weren't at school with me. There used to be a toddler walking by my side of about two and a half years old. I had a three-cornered shawl that I used to wrap round myself, across at the front and knot it and the baby was fixed inside that.

If a child was ill it was all home cures. You just slapped some goose grease on a piece of brown paper and put it on their chests with a piece of red flannel and sweated it out of them. If they had toothache you boiled up some cloves in the water, put them in a bit of cotton wool, soaked it and held it on the tooth, 'til it burnt. If they had earache you boiled an onion and put it in a sock and put it on the pillow and lay on it.

When I was up on the farm there was times when the weather was bucketing down with rain and it had snowed up to the front window. I used to think, 'Oh, God, have I to go through all this again? If only I could have relief from it for a couple of days.' You were never away from your children, from them getting out of bed 'til they went back to bed, they were there the whole time. There was no break from washing, dressing, feeding, cleaning, cooking. When you weren't doing that in the house you were doing the outside work. I said many a time in my married life, 'I'm going to run away,' and I would walk out of the back door, look at the door and think, 'Well, I have no money and nowhere to go so I better go back in.'

As my children got older, I talked to them and told them my worries and troubles. We were surrounded by grass outside. In the summer months we used to go and sit there in the evenings and talk, sing to one another and tell stories. It was a lovely place, was the farm. It was ideal for family because you were your own boss. You could wander where you wanted. We were all countrified. Think of the pleasure when little kids, four or five years old, come in with a bunch of daisies or buttercups and say, 'We picked these for you, Mum.' I didn't ask God or the devil for help to bring 'em up. But they were our life. We loved them and we looked after them. In fact, we worshipped them.

A mother in Eden village in Durham feeds some of her fifteen sons and daughters. In the inter-war years large families were not uncommon in rural areas.

Joyce Bennett

Born in 1917, Joyce Bennett gave birth to an illegitimate daughter when she was twenty-two. Like many before her, she saw her parents bring the child up as their own. She went on to marry Bob and they have three children. They live in South Devon.

Joyce Bennett, pictured as a young girl with her brothers.

When we came out of church on Sunday all these boys used to congregate by the village square just by the pub. The girls would pair off with them. Reg would be there and I'd be dressed up in my hat and coat and gloves. Reg was my first boyfriend – we went to school together – but we didn't start courting until I went into service. He really was my first love. When he said good night there were times when I felt I didn't want him to leave me because I had this funny feeling inside. I felt I was missing out on something when he left. I can remember looking out of the bedroom upstairs and he'd be down on the pavement, shouting out, 'Do you still care for me?' and I used to say, 'Well, I'm looking forward to the day we can be together.' This is what I hoped for because life was so unemotional being in service. Having somebody like that to put their arms around you and hold you so tight, it meant so much to me. I didn't get a lot of affection from my family.

On my days off Reg used to bring me home Sunday evenings. I remember one time we found a hayrick and we went in there and held hands and kissed and cuddled. We were together two or three years before we actually made love. It must have been during the spring, around April, and we wandered down the lane together. It was all very quiet. I was scared in case we had a child. He said, 'It's all right, I'll make sure there won't be any babies.' I had no pleasure whatsoever out of what happened because I was so scared. It was something that he wanted to do and I felt that even though I cared for him this was going a bit too far, to have a sexual relationship.

I realised I was pregnant one morning. My period was overdue. I remember going to the bathroom and I was violently sick. I suddenly realised I must be expecting a child. I was absolutely scared stiff. The first thing I thought about was what Mum and Dad were going to say.

Reggie had arranged to meet me where his father kept some chickens. I was on my way back to the Big House and I remember saying, 'I think I'm in the family way.' He said, 'Oh, you can't be, that's impossible. I have always been so careful, don't blame me.' I think he was scared stiff what was going to happen if his parents found out.

I went back to the Big House, thinking, 'What's going to happen to me?' About a fortnight or so afterwards I went home on my day off. I was talking to my mum and she said, 'Do you know that Reg has left?'

I said, 'What do you mean, left?'

'He's enlisted as an apprentice in the Royal Air Force. He left last week.' There was no way in that day and age you would be allowed to get married in the forces so he took the easy way out. I felt really bitter. Any feelings that I had for him had gone. I really hated him for what he'd done to me.

When the baby started to show I tried to hide it by pulling in my corset ever tighter, which of course made things very uncomfortable. Then one night on my half-day off I had just arrived home on my bicycle. My father came out on the porch and said, *'Who is responsible for your condition?'*

I was absolutely petrified. I said, *'What?'*

He said, *'You're in the family way. Who is responsible?'*

I said, *'It's Reg.'*

Joyce cuddles her illegitimate daughter, Jennifer Megan, who grew up thinking Joyce was her sister.

He said, *'Well, don't stand there for everybody to see you. Get in.'* He said, *'You can't have the baby here, you will have to go in the workhouse. What are people going to say?'*

Well, I felt as if everybody had deserted me. I felt as if I was scum. I couldn't cry. I think it was the shock that Dad had turned against me. I felt as if the whole world was against me. In fact, I think if I'd known a way to do away with myself I would have done. I'd got nothing to look forward to because I'd got this awful stigma on me that I was going to have a baby.

I went back to the Big House and immersed myself in my work to keep busy. I was about five months pregnant when the mistress realised there was something amiss with me. I had been promoted to Cook and she came out and said, *'Are you all right? Is there anything wrong with you?'*

I said, *'Well, I'm expecting this baby.'*

And she said, *'Well then, you can stay with us as long as you feel you can cope with the work but you will have to go home to have the baby.'*

I did go home to have the baby in the end. I'm not going to say my mother and father actually welcomed me home but they accepted me because they didn't like the idea I had nowhere else to go. When the nurse put my little baby in my arms I thought, *'This is mine, this is mine.'* I didn't look to see if she was perfect. I thought I'd got somebody to love and show my affection to because I had so very, very little in my life. My mother came up to see me and said, *'We'll keep her between us and look after her.'* It was such a relief to know I hadn't got to part with her. I felt she was part of me.

We called her Jennifer Megan and when she was about six months Mum said, *'We'll need to get her christened.'* I went to see the rector and said, *'I would like to have my baby christened.'*

He said, *'You're not married are you?'* I said, *'No'*. He said I would have to be churched *(an ancient ritual which 'cleansed' a woman after giving birth)* and told me, 'You have to come and confess your sins because you have this baby and you aren't married. I can't have her christened in the church under the circumstances.'

I was taken by him up to the front pew and I had to kneel down as he was reading these passages out. There were parts of it that I had to repeat, about how awful it was that I committed the sin of having a baby and I wasn't married. I can't remember the exact words but I know it felt as if I had committed a criminal sin.

It seemed to me that it was all my fault and nothing to do with the father of the child and it seemed totally wrong. Even today I can feel the pain and disgrace of having to tell him I was sorry I'd got this baby. I wasn't sorry I'd had this baby, not afterwards, because she was a ray of sunshine into my life.

It never left the rector that I'd had this baby without being married. If he had an opportunity to make me feel small he did. It was the same with the other church members. If I went to church they found some reason not to say 'hello'. I was really the only young girl in the village at that time who was an unmarried mother and to them it was a disgrace, even though I'd gone back to work and did my best to support the child.

Jennifer had been about six to eight weeks old when I was first asked to go back to work. The mistress said they were rather short-staffed – the war had broken out – and they'd lost two or three of their staff. They needed somebody they could rely on. My mum said, 'Well, it's up to you. If you've got the opportunity to get a little bit of money and to help bring up the baby, it would be a great advantage to us.' Going back to work was the only way I could help, even though I was leaving something behind that was part of me.

I had been breast-feeding her at the time and I missed the warmth of having this baby and being able to feed her myself. If it hadn't been for the money my place should have been back home with the baby. I had to work hard and there was no let-up. Occasionally I would go into a little local shop and buy knitting wool and I'd sit and knit for a couple of hours a night. I knitted her a top and a pair of trousers with pale blue bobble wool and I bought a little jacket and she looked really beautiful in it. It was this that has helped me: the fact that I was able to do something for her with my hands, to show the love I'd got for her. I wasn't there when she had her first tooth. Mum would say, 'She started to crawl today.' It was the little things I missed. But I could at least help provide the cash for her milk and for her clothes. I bought her a pram, too, and I can see myself now struggling to bring it home as I cycled with one hand on my bike.

I saw her every other Sunday afternoon and on my half day during the week. It was three and a half miles to my home and it wasn't all plain sailing. There were hills and if the weather was very, very bad there were days I was unable to go back to see my daughter. Halfway through the journey I would see my dad coming up the road pushing the pram and bringing Jenny up to meet me. I used to be able to push her and what a joy it was to be able to take this little baby back home again. But she wasn't mine because she belonged to my parents. They were bringing her up. As she grew older *she began to call my mother 'Mum' and I was Joyce. She was always delighted to see me because as far as she was concerned I was the elder sister. My mother and father really worshipped her; they weren't worried about what the other people outside thought. We were a family and that's what counted most.*

David Spreckley

David Spreckley speaks frankly about sexual ignorance in his boyhood years in the 1920s. In the run up to the war, he joined a commune in London where members experimented with open relationships, part of an attempt to build a better world, free from State control. Although he married during the war, he divorced five years later. No longer a believer in marriage, he has six children by three different women and has been with his present partner for the last forty-five years.

My sex education as a child was absolutely non-existent. I knew literally nothing about sex or puberty. My mother had her lady's maid called Winnie, who was a very shrivelled-up spinster, and on the last day before I went back to prep school she would always come and bathe me. When I was about twelve or thirteen I found that I was growing strange pubic hairs, which I didn't understand at all. But I thought they would embarrass Winnie no end. So before she came into the bathroom I got a pair of nail scissors and started to cut them off. But unfortunately I chose a curved pair of nail scissors and I nipped my skin, so that by the time she arrived the bath was blood red.

David Spreckley as a naïve youth here in the early 1930s.

I didn't kiss a girl until I was seventeen. I just used to go to dances with them up 'til then. When I got to Sandhurst I inherited this idea, which was that a gentleman – and I regarded myself as a gentleman – didn't jump into bed with his girl-friends. If he wanted he went and bought it and that's what I did. I used to get on a coach on Saturday and come up to Piccadilly Circus, where all the tarts were standing, and find a prostitute, which cost me £1 a time. I did that about once every four to six weeks.

The very first time I went she gave me the only sex lesson I ever had in my life. I'd never seen a woman's body and when she took off the top half, I saw her tits. Oh, I was terribly excited. I said, 'Do you give them names?' And she gave them names then, something like Chloe and Cinderella, and then she took off the bottom half and I was absolutely amazed. I didn't know what was there at all and she told me what to do and I did it.

After I left I discovered that I'd left my wallet behind so I went back and walked up about four flights of stairs to her flat. It was at least ten minutes later and there she was. She said, 'Oh, I'm so glad you came. I couldn't wait for you much longer.' And she had waited just so that this poor young boy could get his wallet back.

– Four –

Bitter Harvest

In the 1930s, Ken Walker worked on the family farm in the Yorkshire Dales. His family was in serious debt to the bank and his father was terrified that they would all soon be destitute. Their life, like so many others living off the land, was a constant battle for survival, and one of the greatest worries was the loss of animals through disease. Notifying the authorities resulted in even worse financial disaster as it brought a farm or an entire area under suspicion. Although his own father resisted selling infected beef or milk, Ken remembers that many farmers preferred to keep quiet. As a consequence diseased animals entered the the food chain.

'A common phrase then was "slink", which was low-grade food and mostly from a diseased animal. As soon as a farmer detected that he had a diseased animal, his great ambition was to get shot of it as soon as he possibly could. If they could get away with it and make a profit they considered they were perfectly justified in doing it. If he could get rid of it to a butcher for £15 – well, it was £15 in his pocket. If he left it for a fortnight and sold it to the knacker man or had to bury it – of course, he lost that £15. That was money which kept you clothed and fed and your family clothed and fed. Farmers used to salve their consciences with the attitude that cooking would destroy the bacteria.'

The 1920s and 1930s were decades of crisis in the British countryside. There were many aspects to the agricultural depression, but one of the least documented is the prevalence of animals whose meat and milk were contaminated. Food scares such as 'mad cow's disease' and salmonella poisoning have become so closely associated with the factory farming methods of the post-war years, it is often forgotten that infection from diseased animals was also commonplace in the era of hand-milked cows and small mixed farms. Infected animals were responsible for many deaths from tuberculosis, one of the main life-threatening

A policeman supervises a driver at a farm in Barkway, Hertfordshire as he disinfects his feet to stop the spread of foot-and-mouth disease in 1933.

diseases between the wars. In 1931 alone, over 1,000 children under the age of fifteen died of T.B. in England and Wales through drinking infected milk. Many more were left crippled. In the early 1930s the government estimated that 40 per cent of cows were infected with T.B. There were few legal controls on the quality of farm produce and most farmers could not afford to take any action to combat health problems. As late as 1939, only a tiny percentage of farms in the country had their herds certified free of disease.

British farming had been in decline since late Victorian times, a victim of the nation's commitment to free trade. Cheap wheat and meat, much of it imported from Commonwealth countries such as Canada and New Zealand, had impoverished agriculture at home.

By the late 1930s, British farmers were producing less than a third of the nation's food. The country's 'green and pleasant land' was full of derelict farms, fields overgrown with weeds and neglected hedgerows. In some parts of southern England, where farmers could no longer afford skilled hedgers, the hedges grew to a prodigious height of about twenty feet.

Small mixed farms had increased in number in the early 1920s, when owner- ship of around a quarter of the British countryside changed hands. Many tenant farmers bought the land they worked from their aristocratic landlords, hit by death duties after the First World War. During the war agriculture had enjoyed an upturn in its fortunes when the Government guaranteed prices for crops and introduced subsidies to help boost output. But this brief boom was quickly followed by the Depression. In 1921, all government protection of agriculture stopped and with it, guaranteed prices. Small farmers, who now formed the backbone of British agriculture, found themselves crippled by debts as the Depression began to bite. Few had money to invest in new machinery and age- old methods, little changed for centuries, still predominated.

In the 1920s and 1930s, the horse remained the major source of power on the farm, pulling ploughs, hay-carts and binders. More than 750,000 horses worked on inter-war British farms and the horseman still enjoyed pride of place in the pecking order of farm workers. There were few tractors as early models were quite expensive and unreliable, prone to breakdown and accidents when they turned over on sloping ground. Horses appealed much more to the traditional values of the British farmer; they were extremely cheap during the inter-war years as many town draught horses had been displaced by the advent of motor transport.

This kind of farming was very labour-intensive as many jobs were still done by hand. The high point of the year was harvest time when whole village communities might work together into the night to gather in the crops. Communal work in the fields and closeness to nature were two of the big attrac- tions of farm work during this era. But work on the land, so often romanticized in the past and the present, was very harsh and poorly rewarded. Agricultural labourers were among the lowest paid in Britain. Their wages, an average of £1.50 per week in the 1930s, were a third of those earned by town labourers. Most had a very early start at around five or six in the morning and then had to endure long hours of toil in sometimes bitterly cold, windy conditions. They had no proper or paid holidays. Even on traditional holidays such as Christmas and Easter, there was work to be done feeding animals and checking that the farm was in good order. In some areas the husband and wife were hired together and the wife was expected to work for a pittance or for nothing alongside her husband. The farm workers and their families often lived in 'tied cottages', owned by the farmer who employed them, and their labour was expected for the right to live there. In Northumberland, this was known as the bondager system, or 'the hinds', and survived into the inter-war years. Mary Emerson and her farm worker husband were hired regularly this way.

'Under the system a man and his wife were hired for one year. My husband got 30s a week and I got 5s for milking five cows night and morning and other jobs as well: I spread muck, I cut thistles, picked potatoes, pulled turnips. If the farmer wanted you, you could stay on another year or you could leave. When we left the tied cottage, all our furniture was piled on to a wagon and taken to the next farm we were moving to. We had no idea what kind of cottage we were going into. You'd go and see it and you had to live there, however awful it was. You just tried to make it habitable. Work started the same day.'

Farmers relied heavily on cheap labour all year round. Young farm servants were paid a very lowly wage to do all the menial tasks in the farmhouse and the farmyard. Women were traditionally drafted in to help with seasonal tasks in agricultural counties such as Lincolnshire, where their work included setting potatoes between March and May, cutting cabbages from May, and potato picking in the autumn. Women would toil as their children played in the fields or slept soundly in prams.

Women gathering onions to earn extra cash for the family budget. The cheap or free labour of women played a vital part in the old farm economy.

Farmers could depend, too, on the army of migrant labour that descended on the countryside every spring and summer when there was work to be done. Each year around 100,000 Irish men and women came over to harvest potatoes and sugar beet crops in Scotland, Yorkshire and the East of England. In Yorkshire they were affectionately nicknamed the 'July Barbers' for their hard work in 'shaving' the land. And every autumn there was a mass exodus of 250,000 people from the East End of London to the hop-fields of Kent. The six-week stay in the hoppers' huts was the nearest thing to a holiday most of the families would get. Though the wages were low, they provided a lifeline for poor families who used them to buy a new set of clothes to last the next year. There were also roving itinerants as well as communities of travellers who lived on the edge of villages and spent some of the year in search of seasonal employment on farms. Although there was a demand for casual labour in most rural areas during harvest time, employment might be only for a few days or weeks.

Between the wars, hop-pickers like these travelled from the East End of London to the Kent hop-fields for a working holiday.

Those who worked on the land had to endure not just very low wages but also some of the worst housing conditions in Britain. With an impoverished rural economy there was little or no money for housing improvements. By the inter-war years most of the country housing stock was over one hundred years old and was rapidly falling into disrepair. Families lived in tiny cottages that were dark, damp and had low ceilings. Many were vermin-infested. The lavatory was usually a primitive affair made up of a wooden seat with a hole in it over the earth. There was also an absence of basic public utilities such as piped water and electricity, which by the early 1930s had reached few rural areas. For lighting, families had to rely on oil lamps and candles. Water often had to be collected in heavy buckets from the nearest standpipe, well, stream or river. Even by the late 1930s, less than one farmhouse in six had a piped water supply and in Anglesey it was one in twenty. Some of the worst conditions of all were in rural Wales, where two-thirds of the cottages had been condemned as unfit for human habitation. Olive Morgan, now 85, lived in the small village of Pwll in south-west Wales.

A family living in a pig shed on the outskirts of Woking in 1921. Country people experienced some of the worst poverty in the Depression years.

'I would come downstairs in the morning terrified. I'd make as much noise as I could to frighten the mice away and I put the wireless on to drown out the sound of them squeaking behind the skirting boards. I had to cut my husband's sandwiches every morning sitting on the table because I was afraid to stand on the floor because of the mice and cockroaches. There were cockroaches all over the floor in the morning. Every now and again we'd put powder down to kill them. Well, I'd sweep them up before the kids got up but some would be only half dead. My little one was about fourteen months and he was crawling. I could see him one day sucking something and I said, 'Give it to Mummy,' pulled it out of his mouth and put it in my hand. A cockroach.'

In Northumberland, Mary Emerson and her husband found themselves living in a series of run down and ramshackle tied cottages:

'In one cottage the ceiling was down in the bedroom all the time we were there. The snow used to bleach into the cottage and sometimes even the counterpane of the bed was covered in snow from the attic. There used to be a drift of snow from the door to the fireplace and 'twas the same in the living room. It was all in the loft and when it thawed we had water running all over the place, so we had to have buckets and anything we could lay our hands on to catch the water. It was like that the whole four years we were there.'

There was much pressure on farm labourers and their families to suffer in silence. Invariably, their landlord was also their employer and any dispute could lead to eviction. There was a spate of evictions after the Agricultural Labourers Strike of 1923, the main trade union action of the inter-war years, which unsuccessfully attempted to reverse their falling wages. Even an argument over conditions or the ill health of the labourer could lead to eviction. In 1931, a typical year, the National Union of Agricultural Labourers assisted around 300 of their members who had been evicted.

In 1933 this man was the oldest working wheelwright in Exmoor but the demand for traditional rural crafts was dwindling.

With farming in crisis, unemployment became a major problem in the countryside between the wars. Many farmers had traditionally laid off some of their labourers in the slack winter months: some found work on fishing boats while others went to the towns to look for casual jobs, such as the East Anglian farmhands who traditionally migrated to Burton-on-Trent to work in the breweries. But in the 1920s and 1930s, there were few jobs elsewhere and the periods of unemployment on the farms grew longer. With unemployment sometimes went destitution. Agricultural labourers, deemed too lowly paid to afford National Insurance contributions, were not eligible for unemployment benefit until 1936. Many thousands were thrown on to parish relief, some ending up in the workhouse.

Hard-pressed farmers found themselves laying off workers and working on the land as hard and long as their employees. On smallholdings the success of the farm heavily depended on the skill and efficiency of the farmer's wife in making butter and selling it along with cream and eggs at the local market. Although prices and profits were low for the farmer, a small mixed farm could at least produce enough meat, milk and vegetables to feed the family. What protected many families from the worst ravages of the Depression was the subsistence nature of much of the farming economy. Many farm labourers enjoyed a good-sized garden to grow their own potatoes, onions, runner beans and greens. Often they kept a pig on their smallholdings. The fat hams and sides of bacon hanging in cottage kitchens were an insurance against hunger in the winter months.

With large families commonplace and many mouths to feed, mothers played a vital role in keeping families alive. The thrifty, resourceful country wife and mother made sure nothing was wasted and everything had a use. All surplus fruit would be made into jam and jellies for the winter; stinging nettles were made into an all year-round tonic; dandelions thrown into salads and sandwiches. Their main aim was to put a hot and appetizing meal on the table every day. They could often perform miracles with the most unpromising items such as a pig's head, a sheep's head and lambs' tails. Those who lived in farming villages near the coast had the advantage of adding seafood to their menu, often collected or caught for free. In the 1930s, Maud Bell, the wife of a cowman and mother of three, lived in the Norfolk village of Thornham, three miles from the sea.

'The children used to get together and go to the beach with their buckets and rakes and get the cockles, mussles, winkles. They used to stab flat fish with spear things on the end of sticks and bring them home still wriggling and we would have to wait until they died before cooking them. I'd chop their heads off and make a lovely meal. One night they brought home these crabs. I'd never had a crab before. I had no idea they should be plunged into boiling water to start with.

I put these poor things in a saucepan of cold water and as they got warm so they pushed, lifted the lid and crawled out. I had the lid of the saucepan and wooden spoon, picked them up and popped them in again.'

Large numbers of labourers migrated into the towns in search of a better life. So, too, did many of the farmers who went broke and left farming altogether. Between the wars, the agricultural workforce declined by around a third, and 250,000 men left the land. The families of those who had once worked in traditional rural crafts, such as master bakers, basketmakers, hurdlemakers and wheelwrights, also joined the exodus away from the countryside. Until the First World War, most villages were largely self-sufficient and might have their own blacksmith, corn miller, carpenter-cum-undertaker, thatcher and tailor. Other craftsmen such as saddlers and wheelwrights might serve several villages. But these trades had been in decline since Victorian times when cheaper, mass-produced manufactured goods arriving from the cities had condemned craftsmen to an increasingly impoverished existence. As farming lay in the doldrums and villagers uprooted and left, demand for their skills dwindled still. Despite the fact that there was also much unemployment in the towns, those lucky to find a job enjoyed better wages and more leisure time. Thanks to better communications such as the wireless and cinema, young country men and women were becoming more and more aware of tempting consumer goods such as fashionable clothes and motorbikes. The decline in the rural workforce was

Village carriers like this one in Petworth, Sussex in 1931 were a godsend to wives and mothers in isolated farms and hamlets.

most evident in the southern counties: men were drawn to job opportunities opening up in manufacturing, including the furniture factories at High Wycombe, the Morris car factory in Oxford and the electrical factories in London's outer suburbs. Many young countrymen simply escaped rural unemployment by joining the armed forces, even before the build-up to war.

By the early 1930s, the crisis in the countryside was so severe that farmers, renowned for their political conservatism, began to protest. Many refused to pay the tithe, an ancient tax levied by the Church of England and equivalent to around a tenth of their annual produce. Prices and profits had fallen so much that the tithe, collected by a much-reviled organization known as Queen Anne's Bounty, was now a severe burden. Handing over money which might make the difference between bankruptcy or survival was intolerable. The tithe wars, which began in East Anglia, soon spread to other parts of rural Britain. Farmers united against police and bailiffs who were called in to sell animals, crops, machinery and furniture belonging to rebellious farmers who refused to pay up.

Angry East Anglian farmers protest against paying the tithe to the Church in the early 1930s.

There were extraordinary scenes of violence as farmers obstructed the bailiffs and gave vent to their feelings, assisted by Moseley's Blackshirts who arrived from the cities to support their struggle. The protest was, in the long term, a success and in 1936 the Tithe Act phased out the tax.

There were other demonstrations by farmers calling for state help. The government responded by introducing subsidies, guaranteeing minimum prices and promoting more efficient marketing. Marketing boards were established, the largest of which was the Milk Marketing Board, set up in 1933. Its formation was prompted by the over-supply of milk as thousands had turned to dairy farming where there was more potential for profit than in growing crops. The Milk Marketing Board began a very successful campaign to sell milk as a health food, especially among children. This was ironic for, despite their best efforts to improve hygiene standards, some of the milk sold was in fact contaminated. Even by the Second World War the vast majority of people in rural areas and smaller towns were still drinking unpasteurized milk.

By the late 1930s, however, there were some signs of modernization and much-needed change in the countryside. Larger and more experimental farms introduced tractors and combine harvesters to increase productivity. But although they increased productivity they accelerated the drift to the towns as less labour was needed. More welcomed by villagers was the provision of utilities such as piped

Children enjoy free school milk in 1937. Despite its promotion as a health food, thousands of children had contracted T. B. through infected milk.

water and the increasing rural electrification schemes. Most popular of all was the building of council houses. Despite the fact that their appearance was often plain and ugly, with little of the charm of the old country cottages, they at least provided more space and better amenities for the families of agricultural labourers. Most important of all, living in council homes they enjoyed much greater freedom from the control of the farmer and the tied cottage, as Maud Bell remembers:

'The council houses were one of the best things that ever happened to the working man. You could work where you liked, you weren't tied to a certain farmer and the master couldn't do as he liked with you. We had all been in little cottages before but these new houses were bigger and brighter. We thought we were living in luxury. There was electricity. Well, we'd always been used to filling lamps and using candles, so to walk indoors and flick a switch against the door – it was wonderful. Before, we used to have a tin bath in front of the fire but when they put in a bathroom the kids was always wanting to be having a bath. It was lovely to have running hot and cold water when before we had an old pump that we got water from.'

Mary Rowling

Mary Rowling got most of her six-month long jobs on Cumbrian farms through the hiring fairs in the 1930s. She married in 1943 and moved to Yorkshire where she still lives.

I'd had a good training as a farm servant on my dad's hill farm in the Dales. I worked very hard there doing all sorts like rescuing sheep on horseback in the blizzards. We had no water laid on so we fetched it from a little spring two fields away. I had a yoke shaped around my shoulders with long chains at the side and two old-fashioned zinc buckets attached. I made seven journeys across the fields in the morning and then in the afternoon carrying these very heavy buckets to make sure there was always plenty of water for the cows, housework and washing days. My dad had very bad eyesight and very big, knuckly, bony hands and he used to learn me how to turn lambs' front legs round inside their mothers while they were being born, so I got quite a talent for it and neighbours used to send over for me to help with their sheep. When I went into service and was bigger and stronger, I had to do it for the cows.

I was fourteen when I started as a farm servant. I would be expected to get up at five to blacklead all the big farmhouse ranges and get the fires going. While the fires were burning up, I'd scrub the farmhouse floor and then when the fire were far enough I'd get the kettle on and a big pan on the side for the porridge and cook breakfast for about seven o'clock. They would come in from the milking, then I'd do the washing-up and prepare the dinner, peeling a big bucket of potatoes. The first farmhouse I went, I were peeling potatoes, chopping away, and the farmer's wife said, 'Aye, you've made a good job of them, Mary. Now get your knife again and peel all the peelings because you've wasted half the potatoes with those thick peelings.' She made me peel the peelings to get the shavings out that I had wasted. So it learned you not to waste anything. At another place they had a big black oak staircase and I used to have to make my own polish. I'd scrape all the goo out of the insides of the beehives and mix it with turpentine with a pestle and mortar, a teaspoon at a time. It took all evening, pummelling it and getting it smooth so you could use it for polish.

There were jobs to do outside, too. I'd let the chickens out and feed them in the morning and feed the calves. Then I'd put the milk through a separator if it were a butter farm, or if it were a tuberculosis-tested dairy farm I had to put it through coolers and pressurizers to treat the milk. There were all the dairy utensils to scrub and sterilize. Then you had to go and make the dinner. Every minute was spoken for. I had once a fortnight off after I was sixteen and twice a week when I turned eighteen. At one farm the boss and me caught jaundice from some calves he bought at auction. I was shut off on my own and felt very sickly, unbalanced and me eyes and fingernails were all going yellow. The wife said, 'You can't just lie there.' So she used to bring buckets of potatoes up and a knife and a bucket of water, and had me peeling potatoes sat up in bed and chopping cabbage on a bread board. You hadn't time to be poorly.

A woman carries water with a yoke in a Scottish village. These traditional implements were still being used between the wars as a quarter of all parishes had no running water.

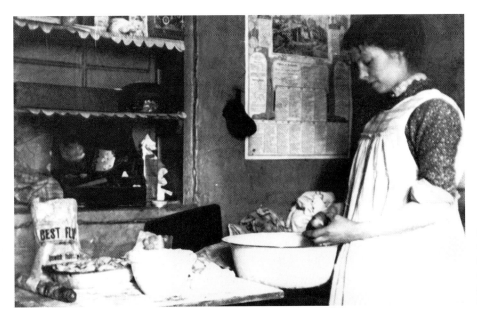

A Suffolk house-
wife prepares an
evening meal
using vegetables
grown in her
cottage garden.

Some of the farmers were quite decent, I'll give them their due. There used to be about six to seven farm men and just the one farm girl hired to live in, and if they saw them taking the mickey out of you or bullying you they wouldn't stand for it. Another time you'd get about as an unhappy family as what I had left behind me.

They used to test your honesty in the farmhouses. I can understand, in a way as you were living in their homes. I used to get down with a hand brush and a little dust-pan on the floor and I would find a sixpence, a shilling, sometimes a florin [a silver coin, worth 2s or 10p] just 'accidentally on purpose' placed under the bed. So I got the idea that I'd use my clog nails, little t-shaped nails, put them over the coin and hammer them into the floorboards so hard nobody could ever get them out. If they left us a three ha'penny stamp, a great thing in those days, I'd lick it and put it flat down where it was. Gradually they got the message and gave up doing those tricks.

When they were hiring you they made a great thing of saying you'd eat off the same table as the boss but you learnt to take that with a pinch of salt. The reality was the farmer and his wife sat at one end of the table, by the fire, and there was the lace tablecloth on, the best china out and the cake in a nice glass stand. At our end, nearest the kitchen door where it was draughty, there was newspaper for the cloth and enamel mugs and bannocks with margarine on. Bannocks were like old-fashioned scones with no sugar in, only flour and water and a bit of a home-made plum jam.

There was this one right big mansion house, rolling in money were the farmers. They wouldn't feed us on our night off and it were seven miles to cycle to the village so where did they think we'd get our supper when we had to work all week? They used to put a big padlock on the pantry door so we couldn't eat food when they were in bed.

After it happened the first couple of times we thought, 'We're not putting up with going to bed hungry.' Me and the servant boys had a real good talk. Ralph, the horseman, suggested that when I cleared the tea table I chucked a loaf of bread and block of butter out of the pantry window. We smuggled out a few plates that weren't often used and knives and forks. We had it all planned out. So when we came in hungry from a night out at the cinema we put our bikes away and scooted off to the cowshed where the cowman was getting the lanterns burning full blast. We put the plates on top of each lamp and then cut great big chunks out of the ham hanging in sacks from the ceiling of the barn and got it sizzling on these plates. After, we stuffed hay back into the ham to make it nice and firm and well shaped. The lads would hang it back again on the beam. The farmer never climbed up there because the hams were kept for haytime; they were a sort of pièce de résistance *for farm workers in the summer. We agreed that we were all leaving at Whitsuntide so nobody would be there to get the blame. We went through six hams while we were there. There was nothing left but the shank, the bone and hay. So light you could throw them up in the air. We hoped they would have a good time with them in the summer.*

John Waspe

John Waspe was born in 1914 and his family had run Woodlands Farm, their 118-acre farm in Suffolk for several generations. Like most farmers they resented having to pay the £50 annual tithe charge and decided to protest.

Tithe protester, John Waspe in the 1930s.

It was the summer of 1932 when the bailiff, along with police and a London company called General Dealers, arrived on our farm. General Dealers were acting for the Tithe Commissioners and they wanted to confiscate our farming implements and sell them off. I was ploughing with our horseman when we had to take the horses off the plough for these men to cart off into a large shed in the meadow. They took the drill, the horse rake, the harrows and cultivator. So we weren't allowed any of our tools to cultivate the land.

But the Waspe family weren't letting it stop at this. Two or three of us went to the shed one night to make our tools useless and unsaleable. One wheel was taken off the drill, one wheel off the horse rake, and the ploughs were stripped and hidden away. Although the police searched the farm and ditches and dragged the ponds, the parts were never found.

Then one morning at about 4am, three or four lorries from General Dealers descended on the farm, along with twenty police officers. A neighbour, who lived opposite the farm, raised the alarm. My father and I weren't fully dressed but we rushed to the farm and two uncles joined us. The men were loading up our implements into lorries, guarded by police. The four of us started to put obstacles in the lorries' path as they had to come through the farmyard on to the road. There was a heap of faggots [bundles of twigs used for fuel] near the farm gate and I started to pile them against the gate but I was bundled away by the police. Arthur, my uncle, felled one. I had a battle with one of the men from General Dealers but we were outnumbered by the police and the raiders. Then I saw my uncle, with a veil on, coming with a box of bees. I grabbed this box of bees off of him and flung it among the police and these raiders. It soon cleared the police off the road. But by this time General Dealers had cut the chain on the farm gate and got out on the road and were away. It was headline news next morning. We carried on working and tilling the land with implements which we borrowed from some kind farmers and were really happy that we were able to bring another harvest in.

At an enforced farm sale a farmer's possessions are auctioned to pay the tithe in the 1930s.

Just before harvest on 19 July the following year, the bailiff arrived on the farm. He was with a number of police officers. We were expecting something like this to happen because we were still withholding payment for the tithe and the sale of farm implements hadn't raised enough money to pay the tithe. Our corn was ready for harvesting and they had come to impound seventeen acres of standing corn. The police put up a tent in one field with three police officers and the bailiff inside so they could mount a guard day and night. Word soon got round, though. The country roads leading to our farm were alive with newspaper reporters and photographers as well as farmers and farm workers who came to support us.

We did have, though, a good relationship with the bailiff and the police, who were all local and sympathised with our protest. The tent they camped in was about a quarter of a mile from the farm gate and all food and drinks had to be left there to be collected by one of the police. We didn't allow the tradesmen or the public to come on to the farm. One day, a tradesman was unloading his goods when I noticed he stuck a crate of beer near the farm gate. I took two bottles of beer out, tipped the beer away and refilled it with water from the horse pond. The water looked just like the brown ale. I went back to the farm gate and slipped these two bottles of water back into the beer crate. The next morning we all heard about it because the police were asking how come two of the bottles they were supplied with contained water instead of beer. They laughed with us over it but I was the only one who knew what happened. From that day on all food and drink had to be guarded all the time by a police escort.

It went on for about ten days but General Dealers had taken on more than they had bargained for. Cutting the corn with a binder and gathering it would have taken a great deal of time and labour, and because the public were so against them they had to withdraw. The headlines in the daily newspapers the next day read: 'Victory for the farmers'. So we were then able to cut the corn, cart it home to our backyard and reap another harvest. We were really happy.

We fully expected something, though, would happen the next year, 1934. We still owed the tithe and the Tithe Commissioners still wanted their money. Other farmers were still holding back theirs and there were demonstrations and other disputes. Another harvest came round and we cut the crops and stood the sheaves of corn in stooks, or shocks as we called them, and just waited and wondered whether we'd get another visit. Sure enough, one morning the police and the bailiff descended on Woodlands Farm. Ten acres of wheat, ready to be carted, was impounded. A tent was set up in this field and put under guard. Newspaper reporters and photographers arrived along with a large number of the public who were filling the roads around Ringshall.

As far as we were concerned, we were fighting for survival and our family. We decided to block both entrances from a field to the road by carting farmyard manure and piling it up in the gateway. There were about nine or ten rows of shocks of corn, the sheaves all neatly tied up with binder string, and we decided to cut the string. Three of the Waspes went up to the field at about ten o'clock on a rather damp and drizzling night. We worked as quietly as possible and crawled from one shock to another to cut the strings. We had to be on alert as the police turned on a searchlight over the field every so often, so when we saw movement in the tent we laid still. It was three or four days before anyone noticed the string had been cut but it put General Dealers' plans back for a week.

Two weeks after, on a Monday morning, all hell broke loose at Woodlands Farm. Scores of police arrived and sealed off all the roads to the farm and surrounding the field. They escorted several lorries belonging to General Dealers which had a large number of men in them. It didn't stop the public from getting on the farm but all they could do was shout and jeer at the raiders. The men from General Dealers' first job was to tie up all the sheaves that had been cut, which took at least three hours. Then they had to load up the lorries. They were ready to move from the field through the farmyard gate when the police noticed a smell of petrol coming from behind a brick wall. We found out afterwards that some member of the public had intended to set fire to the lorries by throwing petrol canisters. So a change of plan was made to leave by a field entrance to the road. My aunt lay down in front of the leading lorry. I was right beside her as a burly policeman picked her up and threw her on one side roughly. A farmer tried to stop the lorry but was treated rough by the police. So the lorries did get away with our corn.

John Waspe's aunt remonstrates with a policeman at Woodlands Farm in 1934.

It was the last demonstration we Waspes made. Questions were being asked in Parliament about how to stop the burden of tithes on the farmers and about the way it was collected and used by King's College and the Church. The general public was surprised that our money went to help educate ministers for the Church and college students. Many of them were sons of members of the House of Lords and MPs.

Marian Atkinson

Marian Atkinson and her husband Bill and their fifteen children lived on Mungean Farm in Cumbria during the 1930s. Bill managed the farm but as he also worked long hours on another farm, much of the work fell on her shoulders.

We were absolutely isolated. We had no other farm round us for at least three to four miles. And the nearest building, Bigland Hall, was about a mile and a half away from us. Oh, we had no news of the outside world because there was no wireless and we never had a newspaper; we would have had to walk two and a half miles to pick one up and we couldn't afford one in any case. I just lived from day to day by what my husband came and told me. He'd tell me who had died, who'd bought a farm and who was moving: little titbits of news.

In the eight years I was at the farm I only left twice – once to go to the hospital where my son was ill and once when my mother bought me a new dress to go to a wedding which I didn't end up going to. What there was of the Depression never reached us because we were self-sufficient. I had my own world. I didn't have to bother with anybody else's, they could do what the devil they liked outside. We just got it into our heads that we were a gang of our own and we lived together, we worked together, we enjoyed life together.

A family bottle-feed some new additions to their Sussex farm in 1934. During the Depression years it was vital to keep every animal alive.

We had no weather forecasts to tell us when it was going to rain or snow but we knew. The sky and the animals were our weather forecast. When we'd got our hay ready for carting, always the night before we went round the field, looked up at the sky, and felt which way the wind was blowing. We'd think, 'Oh, it's going to be a dry night, it's all right, we'll be able to lift this tomorrow.' But sometimes when we went round my husband would say, 'Hark, the sheep are bleating. Oh hell, it's going to rain.' If birds came and sat on my washing-line in front of the house and they faced the gate, it was all right. But if they faced the field at the bottom, it was going to be bad weather. There were always customs we lived with and began to understand.

In the winter and wet weather we used sacks as outdoor clothing. We had miles and miles of binder twine and we tied the sacks around our waists. We made a three-cornered hood out of them, too, to keep our head and the backs dry. Sometimes we had one round our waist, one round our bottoms, one round each knee. The sacks kept us beautiful and warm, they were as good as a top-coat or shawl. It snowed and snowed and snowed in December, January and February. I can remember one morning getting up and the snow was halfway up the windows from the ground up.

We had high walls, at least four to five feet high, to stop the sheep getting out. The sheep huddled together under the walls for shelter when the wind got up. Well, of course, when the snow drifted it buried the sheep. We all carried a crook, a long stick about four feet high with a long crooked end, so that you could put it round the sheep's neck and pull it out. My girls would make a dinner for us while me and my husband trailed around the fields. The sheep made no sound, they were just dumb. We used to scoop the snow with a spade 'til we saw a tail wagging or nose peer out. They used to be frozen to their bodies – white icicles all over the wool. We didn't lose many, two or three, and we ate them. 'Twas good meat and it was like having a deep-freeze because they were frozen. That was another perk we got.

I was the shepherdess the whole time we were on Mungean farm. The lambing season from the end of March to the end of April was bloomin' hard work. I had to go and look at the sheep two, three times a day. I had to get me children to school, get the two or three at home up and washed, dressed and breakfasted, go out to the field to look at the sheep, one child by hand, one in my arms and nine times out of ten, one inside me. I'd tear around, plonk the children under the hedge and go to the ewes in distress who wanted to lamb and couldn't. I used to turn them over on their backs, put my hand up inside them, get the front feet forward and gradually ease it out. The sheep used to be so thankful – you could see it on its face – and she used to 'baa' as if saying, 'thank you'. Probably it had been trying to lamb for two or three hours 'til I got there.

If a ewe died and left a lamb, then it was classed as a pet and it was brought into the house and we bottle-fed it, which the children delighted in doing. They sat by the oven, kept warm. But if a lamb died, I skinned it and put the skin over another lamb so the mother thought it was its own. After a period of about two or three days it would take to that lamb like its own and you could take the skin off.

All the lambs had their tails cut when they were about five or six weeks old. You had to cut them off to keep them clean at the back. They were all put in a bucket, then I took them home and skinned them and cooked them over peat and wood – we had no coal. You put them in a pan with some salt and some herbs and some onion and made a jolly good stew with a handful of barley, a handful of peas and a handful of rice. We only had lambs' tail soup once a year and it was a big favourite. Nothing went to waste on the farm, absolutely nothing.

Occasionally we got a lamb, sometimes once a month. If a stray lamb came you put a notice up: 'Please claim within twenty-eight days'. If nobody claimed it, it was ours. My kids used to say, 'When are we going to have sheep's head broth again, mum?' So we were always on the look out for one. I used to cover it with salt water all night to clean it and get all the mucus out of the mouth and nostrils. I'd take the eyes out but leave the ears on. I covered it with salt water and brought it to the boil and boiled it for sometimes six hours, up on the rail in the pan until the flesh started falling off the bones and then lifted it on to a platter. You pulled all the flesh off the teeth and the jaw bones and the cheek bones. This stock it had been boiled in was kept for soup the next day, to which I added onions, a turnip, carrots and cabbage. The sheep's brains were a delicacy, there were fights over them. They were creamy-coloured, like a lot of little pipes all glued together. They were washed, dried and floured and fried on each side in a pan until they were brown.

A Cornish housewife, pictured in 1936, bakes pasties – the favourite local dish among farm labourers.

A crofter's wife. Some of the most primitive conditions were endured in the remote Scottish islands.

I never had no wages, I worked for the rent and home. The farmer did provide us with some potato seeds and turnip seeds and a piece of ground. We had as much milk as we wanted and I made the cream into butter because I'd been a dairy maid. We grew our own potatoes, onions, carrots, cabbage, kale: everything we wanted. I kept my pantry supplied with food without having to go out of the house. We had a delivery once a month: a hundredweight of white flour, five pounds of yeast and various things like salt and syrup. I baked twenty-eight loaves a week. I bottled fruit, I made jams and preserves and pickles. We grew onions in the garden so I made chutney. We killed a pig of our own and I cured them and hung them on the beams in the dairy with old net curtains round to stop the flies getting on them. I made sausages, black puddings and chitterlings. We had huge pigs, which you could have sat on their backs they were that broad. You got basins and basins of lard out of them.

From May to October or November we went bare-footed. It was a sense of freedom in one way and a sense of saving up in another, because while you weren't wearing your shoes, you weren't wearing them out. It was lovely walking on stone flag floors in the cottage and on green grass with nothing on your feet. The beauty of life was the countryside: the coming out of the leaves in spring after all the bare branches in winter; daisies, buttercups, primroses coming up, the fruit coming on the trees. I liked the summer but it were hard work because we did the hay making and there were potatoes to dig up. But I did like the autumn season. It was a beautiful time of year to be alive. All the leaves were turning different colours. You could go out into the landscape and look at the fields and there wasn't two greens alike. We noticed it in those days, because we had nothing else to distract us. It was our life, was the country.

Duncan Williamson

The descendant of nomadic Scottish tinsmen and basketmakers, Duncan Williamson was born in 1928 and grew up in the forest of Argyll, where the Duke had given his family permission to stay. He spent part of the year working on small hill farms, and the remaining summer months walking the length and breadth of Scotland, firstly with barrow and pram and later with horse and cart.

What I so loved as a travelling man was the freedom. The feeling of being a free-born spirit with all the knowledge and education given to me by my parents, learnt down through the ages. I left home when I was about thirteen. Sometimes I would travel around Scotland with my brother Sandy and his wife and children and later with my first wife, Jeannie. There were lots of travelling families wandering around the country, everybody trying to make a living to the best of their ability. Sometimes there would be fifteen or sixteen families at one camp and we'd sit and share news and stories.

In the early days I took little jobs like working with fishermen and woodcutters and dry-stone builders. I was very well received, especially by the farmers because I did a lot of good work for them: picked the stones off the fields and built the dykes, cut their hay and gathered the tatties and helped them in many ways. I could walk for miles looking for work because on the west coast, the Mull of Kintyre, the villages and towns are few and far between and it wasn't every farmer who had need of you. I'd be soaked to the skin walking. I used to sleep everywhere, maybe in a graveyard shed where the gravedigger kept his tools. I was lucky if I had a job on a farm because I could sleep in the byre among the straw and there's no more comfortable feeling than

A tinker's encampment near Castlebay, Barra in the Scottish isles.

being in a barn among the beautiful corn straw. But I kept myself clean, always, because I'd go to a quiet place where nobody was around and just dive into the sea.

My daddy never owned a horse in his life because he'd no need for one. But I said, 'Some day, when I grow up, I'm going to own a horse.' I used to go to the horse market and see all these beautiful horses getting sold. I saved up a few pounds and bought myself a little horse. I loved that horse. Life was hard for it sometimes, especially in the winter time because grass was scarce. Sometimes I'd have to buy some hay from a farmer or steal a bit at night. No good travelling man would have his tea and go to bed and leave his horse standing without any food. Your horse was the pride of your life. You used your horse like you use a van today. It carried all your possessions. If you were working on a farm you had maybe five miles to go to the village. You needed it to carry your foodstuffs back and sticks for your fire in the winter time. We learned to shoe our own horses. If you didn't have any money you went to a blacksmith and got some second-hand shoes. There was a little blacksmith shop in every village you went to.

Horses were the lifeblood of the country at that time. To have a good trotting horse was a great thing and you wanted it to go faster than somebody else's horse, so you could overtake. Today you have a sports car to show off. Travellers swapped horses all the time. Once you slapped hands there was no way back. You'd hold your hand out and say:

'Come on now, I fancy your horse.'

'Will you give me a fiver?'

A horse fair in Hertfordshire in 1926.

'*No, no! Two pounds.*'

This would go on until a good deal was made. But no travelling man would swap with a woman. Two women could swap horses but not a man and a woman. You'd never be classed a horsy man if you did. It was the custom.

You had to be careful of the kind of horse you bought, especially if you had small kids. It had to be fast and it had to be healthy, it had to be strong and it had to be quiet, free from vice – no kicking or biting. We used to buy a lot of unbroken ponies from Ireland and break them in for saddling. I remember buying one horse and it was so wild I had to put a rope round its neck, throw the rope over a tree, pull its neck up into the tree and climb the tree to get the bridle on that horse. I had it for two years and it became one of the nicest, quietest horses I had ever had in all my life. When we were buying horses we said the wilder the spirit, the kinder the soul.

If a horse was poor in the spring, we knew fine that it had a worm which we could cure ourselves. We used to boil wild broom until it turned green and put a bottle of it down its neck. We starved the horse and would keep giving it bottles until it would pass the worms. Then it would start fattening up. You knew if a horse had worms because it wouldn't cast its coat in spring and it would never fatten up. Some dealers got a good horse cheap that way. They'd tell the owner a lot of baloney that the horse had some complaint: 'I'll take it off your hands anyway,' he'd say and get it cheap. You had to learn all the tricks when you went to a horse market.

I remember a horse market in Perth which started at eight o'clock in the morning and went on until eleven at night, with these people swapping and dealing, hitting hands. You could buy a horse in the morning, sell it in the afternoon and get the same horse back before you left for home at night and you'd maybe end up with a fiver in your pocket. Of course, if a horse was getting old and thin, we'd give it a good feed and then get a couple of tins of baking soda and get it to drink this. When you took it to the market in the morning its belly was all swollen up and it looked like it had a good belly on it. The guy who bought it took it to the stable but the next morning it was standing there collapsed like a penny. They called it 'getting burned'. I was burned many times myself.

After I got married I went to one farm for seventeen years. I went in October and I never left 'til April. The farmer gave me an old cottage to live in and a field to let my horse run free in. I put my first family in the little school and I worked all winter through looking forward to the travelling. We had spring fever. I couldn't wait until spring came to take my kids off to travel, show them a bit of the country, camp in different places beside little streams. I'd take them by the sea and to places I'd been as a kid and teach them things I'd learnt. The travelling culture did not understand this need for a steady job. The meaning of life for a traveller is out there on a summer's morning, your horse by the head, his belly full, your belly full. We'll see new places, we'll be on new roads, we'll travel far and we'll enjoy life.

Joan Rogers

Born in 1914, Joan Rogers grew up in a house with two acres in Billericay in Essex. An idyllic childhood instilled Joan with a love of rural life which led her to take up farming during the 1930s. She spent forty years in dairy farming and was a prize-winning herdswoman.

Joan Rogers with one of her beloved cows.

I fought my family tooth and nail to get on the land. My mother loved the country but she didn't want me to take up farming. She thought it a dirty, unladylike job. I suppose it was because women were doing the sorts of jobs they wouldn't normally do like getting the cows served by the bull. It wasn't done, you see.

At fifteen years of age they sent me to a convent in Belgium – a finishing school – but I didn't finish much. I ran away and hid for four days in the sheds. I was so unhappy and rebelled as I was coming up to be sixteen and wanted to be free. I didn't want to stay in the convent and learn to be a lady. I wanted to get out into the air and be on a farm among the flowers and trees and the animals. And I meant to do it.

My father said, 'She's got to come home. She's got to be given a chance now to show what she thinks she can do with animals. She'll possibly hate it. Let her winter and summer it.' They thought if I had it hard enough on a farm in the wind and the rain and cold and wet I would get the stuffing knocked out of me. But, of course, it was just the reverse.

I started as an apprentice herdswoman for two lady farmers. Of course, some of it was an eye-opener. When Miss Lomax, the younger one, asked me to go down the cowshed cesspool I nearly died. You had to get down in wellies on a little iron ladder and clear out the blocked drainway pipe. I said, 'I'm not going down there, not for all the gold in the world.' She just took no notice at all, but tied a sack round her waist, got down into the cesspool and cleared it out. In her very quiet voice she said, 'Next time, when I ask you to do a job you do it because I never ask a pupil of mine to do a job that I haven't done myself.'

It was a mixed herd I learnt to start with – shorthorns. There was this rapport with cows that I found you could have. I knew people had this with horses but people never thought to make a great fuss of cows. They would think they were dirty, uninteresting animals but they're not, especially when you move into pedigree cattle. They always answered a special call. It would possibly be about five o'clock in the morning. They would be a long way away but it would be near to their milking time and they knew this so you'd get as near as you felt like walking and you'd shout 'C-o-o-m, c-o-o-m, come along!' And they'd come.

My little favourite was Daisy, a red and white shorthorn, and she really loved me. I used to make chicken mash and mix it up into a few snowballs and put it on the top of the bucket as I passed through the cows' field. I used to have a special call, 'Come on, Daisy,' and she would come running and I'd stuff one of these into her mouth. Well, the others got the idea that she was getting something they hadn't got so they all started to come and I would be bombarded and they'd knock the bucket down off my arm and take the contents. My boss stopped it as I was in the middle of these milling cows and she thought I might come to harm. They knew the grub was coming. It was love and food, food and love!

When the cows had eaten their food and they'd been cleaned and swilled down, the next routine would be milking so they expected to have a wet cloth sloshed on the udder. You would wash the teats and the bag. By the time you finished twenty to thirty cows, the first one was quite dry and ready for milking. It was Grade A milk and I'd be in my white milking gear: a white coat, Wellington boots which had to be scrubbed before to make sure there was no muck on them and a hat. I'd take the stool, pop it under me and put the bucket between my legs at the same time, put my head on the flank and I always used to milk the back quarters first. You used to use all sorts of words when you trained them. I used to say, 'Come on, get over,' and they'd get over so you could put the pail of water by the front legs. It was the same as working and talking to heavy horses.

Some people used to tell me I fussed too much but I considered that the more fuss you made with them the more they got to like you. They were happy and contented when you were milking because they can withhold their milk – sort of clench the muscles in their udder: you can pull and pull until you're blue in the face, you never get any milk, with or without machines. I found it most satisfactory if I could get more milk from a certain cow than someone else could – a bit of conceit there.

I loved to groom a pedigree herd. I always liked to polish the horns. You would get a sliver of glass and scrape a sliver off of the covering of the horn and then you cleaned it, rubbed it over with oil and, of course, they shone. They looked beautiful and at Christmas time I used to hang holly in the baskets up in the cowshed and decorate the stalls. At one place I tied ribbons around their neck but the employer wasn't very happy about that.

One of the great joys of my job was when the cows were giving birth. I used to get very excited as she got near her calving. I used to take care of them like patients in a hospital. They didn't like people there, especially anybody they didn't really know so I would allow nobody to look over the door when an animal was giving birth. I was the only one that went near them.

Milking by hand at a St. Ives farm. For many, the close relationship with farm animals was one of the great joys of their work.

I always remember my first breech birth. The vet decided it would have to be pulled out with ropes so I set about disinfecting them, with another girl. He said, 'Anybody around but you lasses?' Well, I wasn't going to have the men in on this so I said, 'No one else around, but don't worry we know our job. When you say pull, we pull.' A lovely heifer calf appeared, which seemed dead to me. The vet grasped both back legs and held it upside down, while I opened its mouth to remove the mucus. He then laid the calf down and blew into its open mouth. There was a splutter and a gasp and I shouted, 'It's alive!' The mother started licking and murmuring to her new baby. It's a sound which you never hear, ever, except when a cow has had a calf.

I used to feel exhilarated, I really did. The calf would keep falling down so I used to have to kneel down and rest its body on my knee and try to make it hang on to the teat. Once it did that you were home and dry. I used to look over the door and feel the most tremendous satisfaction of a safe birth which I'm sure is what people feel with humans, but I always felt this very strongly with animals.

Early on in my career I got engaged to my brother's best friend who I had known for some time. He would come down to the farm and help me with the jobs I had to do so that I got off early and we could go out together. He was always talking about getting engaged and in the end, to keep him quiet, I thought I'd better say yes. It was a terrible thing to do really because in my heart of hearts I knew I wouldn't give up farming and my beloved cows to be married to what I called a city slicker. I thought, 'I shall have to live in a town in a line of houses; there won't be fields, there won't be trees and the bird-song in the morning.' He kept talking about the future and I thought, 'I've just got to get out of this.' I did it in the most appalling way. It was the worst thing I ever did in my life. I wrote him a letter because I knew otherwise he would talk me round again because he was very strong-willed. I put his beautiful diamond and opal ring in a matchbox and sent it with a long letter. I said I was so sorry that I had to break his heart, which I felt I was doing, but I wouldn't make him happy. I had a greater love for cows and all the time I would want to get back to be with my animals; they were my family.

Ernie Gray

Ernie Gray, born in 1912, was a farm worker in the Cambridgeshire Fens during the Depression. Now a widower, he still lives in rural Cambridgeshire.

My father was a horseman and he learnt me all the tricks of the trade. It didn't matter what the job was, it was just horses until the tractor come along. And everybody took pride in their work, especially the way the horses looked, the way they acted, the way they were treated, how fat they were, what condition they were kept in. Everybody had as much pride in that as they did in their own home, oh yes.

I never had no lady friends at that time so all I'd got to look forward to was my mates, my horses. If I went to the field they'd come to me to nuzzle me as much as to say 'Hello, how you getting on?' When I used to go to the stables to take 'em in every morning I would give 'em a holler or a whistle and they'd come trotting up to me and I'd take 'em through the front gate and go through into the stables. They were like sheep nearly. They'd come in and get in the right order when they went in the stable.

To us we knew the horses, we could talk to'em. If we went to plough or harrow or drill, we had words and sounds. If you wanted to go right you'd make a noise like

During the 1930s, most farmers still used traditional methods of horse and hand. In the depths of winter ploughing was far from romantic.

'wutch' and they'd turn to the right a little and if you wanted them to go some more, you'd tell 'em again. If it was go left then it was 'come 'ere' and then they'd go straight on again. You'd have a straight line behind you when you got to the other end of the field. You would be at it for days and days and days, ploughing your field one furrow at a time. You'd have to walk behind the horse all day and you perhaps wouldn't see a soul in the Fen all day. You'd stop about half past ten, have a half hour off for docky – as we called our snack – and then off you'd go again. I imagine I walked twenty, perhaps thirty mile a day. It was a terrific distance from seven to three or four o'clock.

Oh, the weather was terrible at times. If a high wind got up when the weather was really rough and blowy, that'd pick up some of the earth up from the ground and blow it up in terrific clouds. You'd hardly be able to see twenty yards sometimes when they were really, really rough. You wouldn't be able to breathe. There were times when we had to have two or three days off because of the stifling dust. You wouldn't get no money for it. But there were times you had to work regardless of the weather. Snow, ice, rain – freezing – but you'd have to put up with it. You dressed as well as you could by putting on an overcoat or an old bag tied round yer waist, that would have to be your cover and your warmth. If you didn't work, you didn't get paid, as simple as that. Everything was done by hand, we even used to drill the onions and carrots by hand – one row at a time. You'd walk about twenty miles a day, a nice gentle, but steady walk. You wouldn't be able to stop, otherwise there would be a gap in your seeds, so you'd have to keep walking the whole time unless you hit a stone. It could take you two or three days to do it.

Things got really hard, though, in the Depression. I'd been married a few years. Jobs were few and far between. I tried everything; I'd go on my poor old bike to different places like a farm where they'd got a couple of fields. But I'd be told 'We don't want no help, we ain't got no jobs.' I'd perhaps get a job for a week, get a little bit of money in my pocket, and then go somewhere else and look for another job. We had to bodge here and bodge there and see if we could get hold of something to keep us ticking over. It was the most hurtful thing to think that you couldn't earn money to look after your wife and pay your way.

I was agile as any man could be, nimble and hard-working. All I wanted was the opportunity to work but there just wasn't the work about. The parish council found me a job a time or two while I was a hardship case – helping to mend the roads or drive a lorry or cart a few stones or sand. But you got very little for it. I was an agricultural labourer and in them days there was no dole for us. Land workers didn't count.

In the village we lived in a council house. The rent was 5s a week but we were short of money. We couldn't buy all the groceries so we had to go on parish relief for six months or more. You couldn't be anything else but ashamed of it but if you didn't have that you couldn't live. I was afraid to face people. I was ashamed to go into the shop. You went in with a bit of paper from the council and said the things you wanted. The shopkeeper would give you your bread and cheese or whatever. If you were lucky you got a bit of butter or a sausage.

While this was going on I could see my wife's health gradually going downhill. I could see by her manner, by her talk, she was getting very, very much downhearted. I was afraid that if we weren't careful she would have a nervous breakdown. I came close to one myself thinking 'Am I going to stick it, am I going to be brave enough to carry on?' I tried fussing on her, tried loving her – I did love my wife very much. I had a big fear that I was going to lose her to a mental home and if I lost her whatever would I do. But I thought 'For heaven's sake boy don't give up.' I used to tell myself 'Get up and do something, get her going, get her into good health'.

So I tried my best and then at the finish we got this other job on a farm and my wife picked up. We never looked back. We had thirty years there. The farmer got rid of a lot of the men as time went by. The old guv'nor lashed out with everything mechanical. We used to drill beet with a tractor – carrots, onions, everything – and we used to take everything up with a tractor. I'd already learnt how to drive one years back. The wife got so she could drive a tractor, too. She would come with her tractor and trailer and catch the corn I'd combined, put it straight into the truck, take it up to the carts and put it in, and load it into a big wagon and they'd come and take it down to the factory. The farmer, me and her used to manage 130 acres between us.

It was strange to think in the first years horses was your life, you had to work them to live. Then as the years went by you had to work the tractors to live. You couldn't find a horse in the Fen hardly. With the tractor you hadn't got no walking to do, you was riding in comfort all day long and sitting pretty. As things got more mechanical you got better wages because you was more responsible. The less work you'd got, too and you felt a better man because you wasn't tired when you went home. Perhaps you'd have the evening playing cricket, do a bit of gardening or perhaps get on your bike and go to the pictures. You could live at home after you'd done your day's work and you were raring to go the next morning at seven o'clock as if nothing had happened.

The tractor was the biggest godsend that ever anybody could have. We thought we was really rich – for our way of life anyway – because we'd had all them poor years. To have the tractors and get a good wage we was as happy as all the birds in the air.

Tractors, like this one pictured in 1929, were a rare sight on farms between the wars. Many farmers viewed them as five-minute wonders.

– Five –

Forgotten Front Line

In November 1940, a bomb scored a direct hit on the thatched cottage of Fred Austin who was living there with his young family and parents. The beautiful house in the Northamptonshire village of Titchmarsh had been in the family for generations. Fred, then thirty-two, recalls:

'We were woken by a sudden light in the bedroom. We ran into the garden and you could see the sheep's eyes all of a glow from the glare of incendiary bombs that were falling. Then I noticed that one bomb had lodged itself on a bone-dry old beam in the cottage. I put water on it but that made the fire worse, it loved water. I should have used sand. I quickly got the family out and we

Barbed-wire barriers are put in position near the south coast to halt the expected invasion in summer 1940.

watched as the roof caved in. We waited and waited for the fire-brigade and when they came I could have cried. It was too late, there weren't twenty stones left to rebuild it with. It was just rubble and we had to move away. My father never got over the loss and he died shortly afterwards.'

The impact of the Second World War was as dramatic in the countryside as in the cities. It has often been assumed that air attacks only hit urban targets, but farms, villages and market towns also suffered heavily. Rural Britain played a vital role in the war effort. It housed hundreds of thousands of evacuees, it gave up land for many crucial army and air bases and, most importantly, it fed the nation for five years when food supplies were desperately short. To begin with, however, deep-seated divisions between the country and the city, and villagers' suspicion of change, created problems for the government's plans for a nation at war.

In the fraught months following the outbreak of war in September 1939 there was a mass exodus of around three million people from British towns and cities considered vulnerable to enemy air attacks. The countryside was seen as a safe haven away from the heavy bombings that were predicted in major cities such as London, Birmingham, Manchester, Leeds and Glasgow. Most school-age children, clutching their bundles of belongings and boxed gas masks, were evacuated by train and coach as part of hastily organized government schemes. But although the newsreels showed smiling children happily settling into their new country homes, things were not going according to plan. When the children arrived at their country destinations, the billeting system sometimes broke down and a kind of 'slave market' developed in village halls, with bewildered children being inspected like cattle. Many of the children from slums were lice-infested and strangers to washing. In many instances nobody wanted to take them. Even when they found a home the street-wise children often horrified the 'receiving families' with what they regarded as uncouth behaviour. Swearing was a common complaint. For many of the children, unnerved by the strange sights and sounds of the countryside and sometimes treated like second-class citizens in their new homes, it was a distressing experience. By December 1939, when the mass bombings predicted by the government had not materialized, many of the evacuees returned home. Of the three quarters of a million evacuated from London, over half were home by Christmas.

In the early summer of 1940, rural Britain found itself in the front line. When the British Expeditionary Force was evacuated from Dunkirk and France surrendered, invasion of Britain became a very real possibility. Nowhere was the threat felt more strongly in the countryside than in the south-east, especially the coastal regions where Hitler planned to land his troops before advancing to London. Countrymen and women all over Britain were warned to be vigilant for suspicious strangers in the village who might be fifth columnists passing on secret information about the locality to enemy forces, and for German parachutists who might land in empty fields. Spies and saboteurs were popular topics of conversation in village pubs and outlandish stories sometimes started. One rumour had it that German paratroopers disguised as nuns were going to fall from the skies with weapons hidden under their habits. Signposts were taken down in case they might help the invader or spy, and church bells were silenced, to be rung only if or when the invading forces were approaching British shores.

It was in this climate of fear that the Local Defence Volunteer force was formed in May 1940, re-named the Home Guard by Churchill just a few weeks later. Despite its 'Dad's Army' reputation for amateurish antics, the Home Guard took its duties seriously. At first, units were comprised of motley crews, sometimes made up of teenage boys and ageing World War One veterans armed with pitchforks. But as the war went on, more sophisticated equipment became available and the Home Guard developed into a mobile defence force better able to offer resistance in a possible invasion. In the countryside the units were often made up of farmers, farm workers, blacksmiths, postmen and station masters. They already worked long, hard hours but they sacrificed their free time, attending regular drills in village halls, farm buildings and the squire's land. There were frequent military manoeuvres. Many hours were spent training

A military exercise taking place in a Kent village, 1940.

outside, crawling through undergrowth, spending nights in barns, erecting roadblocks. Hidden all over the countryside were pill-boxes disguised as haystacks and underground bunkers from which they would set up defensive positions if the invasion started. Many villages were fortified. Mock invasion drills were carried out with other villages, and men were trained in the use of mortars, flame-throwers, and sub-artillery.

It was the countryside that felt the first impact of German air attacks. The first civilian to be killed in an air-raid was a countryman in the Orkneys, who died on a moonlit night when he attempted to rescue a woman neighbour whose farmhouse had been bombed. During the summer of 1940, the first major air battle to occur in the war, the Battle of Britain, was fought over the south-east counties. Hitler's invasion plans hinged on destroying British airpower first. Worst hit in the raids that followed were counties such as Kent where there was a concentration of RAF bases, including Biggin Hill, Hawkinge and Lympne, that were targets for enemy bombing. Quiet villages suddenly found themselves in the centre of the action as dog fights were fought overhead, aircraft crashed, farm workers were fiercely assaulted as bombs rained down – some of them misdirected from military targets.

Mothers and their children watching a dogfight over the hop-fields in Kent in August 1940.

The success of the RAF in the Battle of Britain forced Hitler to postpone his invasion. But a new horror was in store as he now sought to terrorize the civilian population into submission – the Blitz. In the autumn of 1940, bombs were dropped on many British cities, and semi-rural counties on the *Luftwaffe*'s flight path from France were vulnerable too. On 10 November, a peaceful Sunday morning in the Kent village of Swanscombe was shattered when a missile dropped by raiders making for East London hit a packed pub with a deafening explosion heard for miles around. Twenty-seven people lost their lives. Around a year later, the tiny settlement of Sturry, near Canterbury, became the most devastated village for its size in the country, when two parachute bombs were dropped in the main street killing fifteen people. The impact of these bombings was all the greater because of the small size of the communities and because most people had always assumed they would be safe. Although blackout precautions were followed and air-raid sirens sounded, many people had no shelter to go to when enemy planes were overhead and resorted to sheltering under stairs or even in cut-out corn stacks. Even when shelters were provided, some like VAD (Voluntary Aid Detachment) nurse Pleasance Bett, brought up on a Norfolk country estate, refused to use them.

'These big bombers would come and the siren would go, sometimes by day and sometimes by night. We were all supposed to get out of bed and go into the shelter. Well, having had a heavy day's work, to get out of bed and go and prop myself up on somebody's shoulder on a hard seat in an enclosed cavern, it didn't suit me. Next time we had an air-raid siren I got into the wardrobe. I thought, "If I'm going to panic, I will panic alone and not in a shelter." So I always went in the wardrobe. Most sensible, but I didn't tell anybody.'

The Blitz on the cities between autumn 1940 and spring 1941 brought a new flood of evacuees into the countryside. Many thousands trekked out to seek the relative safety of rural areas, pushing handcarts and babies in prams. Most slept rough in fields, under hedges or in barns. Some families even began living in caves. Fleeing Londoners discovered a series of caverns at Chislehurst in Kent and broke into them. After a week of the Blitz, more than 8,000 Londoners were living there. To begin with, families slept on the stone floors; then after several weeks beds, armchairs and tables were transported down in carts and lorries. Similar patterns of cave dwelling developed close to several other badly bombed cities. Hundreds of Bristol families moved into the Portway caves beside the River Avon, while a few journeyed down to the caves in the Cheddar Gorge.

There were also many unofficial evacuees from the picturesque towns that were the target of Hitler's 'Baedeker raids' in the spring and early summer of 1942. The *Luftwaffe* set out to destroy some of England's most beautiful towns,

Weary townsfolk tramp across the fields to find shelter in the forest after severe raids on Plymouth in May 1941.

listed in the *Baedeker Guidebook* and noted for their historic architecture: Exeter, Canterbury, York, Bath and Norwich were all targeted and effectively blitzed, costing more than a thousand lives. Les Cox, like many others, was stunned when Bath found itself under siege. He and his parents would retreat to fields near their bungalow on the outskirts of Bath when the air-raid siren sounded. One night, a few hours after they had already trekked out, the weary family decided to shelter under one bed instead:

'As I was going under, the bomb hit us. It was a sensation of being steam-rollered, I wanted to take a breath and couldn't and felt light-headed and floaty. Then I realized I was completely pinned, lying on my face, trapped under debris. I heard my mother call out , 'Ollie!' – my father – and with that there was silence. I twisted my head round and could see the roof flickering with flames. Through sheer panic and strength given to me from somewhere I pulled myself free. I tried to feel for my parents but there was nothing but rubble. I ran out and the planes were machine gunning along the wood. A bullet grazed the top of my head and I stumbled and lay down in the field. My left arm was a dead weight, my collar bone damaged and blood was pouring from my face. I knew my parents were dead.'

By this time evacuees of all kinds were being accommodated in a much more friendly and effective way. Emergency services in rural areas provided blankets and soup kitchens to those sleeping rough. The caves where people sheltered were made safe and more comfortable. By 1942, the Chislehurst caves boasted bunk beds, canteens, a children's chapel and a cave hospital, and the billeting system for children evacuated under official schemes was much improved. The nightmare of the Blitz and the shared suffering of the war brought out a more generous, communal spirit in country people. More and more evacuees were beginning to enjoy their new country childhood and every summer they helped the farmers bring in the harvest. For some, it would foster a life-long love of the countryside.

It was not the Blitz, however, but the war at sea that was to have the deepest impact on country life. During the first years of the war, German U-boats achieved devastating success in sinking British merchant shipping. They prevented the arrival of cheap imported food from the Empire, upon which Britain had become dependent for most of her needs. Farming, which had long been in decline, suddenly had to be mobilized for essential food production.

From the beginning of the war, the government took control of the nation's farms through a network of War Agricultural Committees. They helped initiate the beginning of an agricultural revolution in the countryside. Their first priority

Bath residents rescue their valuables from their bombed homes in April 1942.

A new type of spraying machine uses chemicals to destroy fruit tree pests in Cambridgeshire in December 1942.

was to increase production of essential crops such as wheat and potatoes. Farmers were given the financial backing to plough up pasture land, pull down hedges, use artificial fertilizers, keep fewer livestock and cultivate marshland, swamp and old fields that had returned to nature. In the Fenlands, thousands of acres that had never been cultivated before were drained and brought under the plough. Celery and corn grew where there had once been bogs and reeds. To achieve all this, machinery, such as the huge excavators which cut out drainage channels, was used on a hitherto unimagined scale. There was encouragement and pressure to buy tractors, too. The number of tractors in Britain increased from about 50,000 in 1939 to over 200,000 by the end of the war. By 1943, record harvests were being reported as the land became more productive than ever before.

Those farmers who failed to achieve the targets set by the ministry were dispossessed. The War Agricultural Committees compiled what was described as a modern Domesday book, listing every farm in the land and classifying them as 'A', 'B' or 'C' according to merit. Around 5 per cent of farms were given a 'C' classification and if they failed to improve, the War Agricultural Committees then took over and the farmer was evicted without compensation. There was no right of appeal. Fifteen thousand farmers suffered this fate, many complaining, with some justification, that they had been treated harshly and were victims of local vendettas.

In May 1941, a farmer at Malmesbury was given only six days to leave the land he had farmed for thirty-five years. Perhaps the most controversial case was that of George Walden, an elderly Hampshire farmer who barricaded himself in his farmhouse with a gun after being served with an eviction order for refusing to plough up his land. Armed police were sent in and he was shot dead resisting arrest. The distress of such events caused several suicides to occur among dispossessed farmers. In 1941, Angela Aldington and her parents were ordered to leave the Elizabethan farmhouse and land her family and forebears had farmed in Warwickshire for more than 100 years. Now a farmer herself, she recalls:

'We were good farmers and we knew our land. Dad wouldn't plough up the land the War Agricultural Committee wanted for potatoes because it was too boggy and he'd nearly gone bankrupt trying to drain it before. Not only was the order stupid, it was a financial impossibility. It was deeply traumatic for Father and he never came to terms with it. At the time of the farm sale he was in bed with pleurisy and pneumonia. All the furniture and animals had to go. It was heart-breaking. We were homeless but relatives put us up in a tiny house in Redditch. I learnt after that, all through the war not a single potato was planted on that land. But all through my life I always felt the stigma of our family being branded bad farmers.'

The mobilization of the land required a new army of labour to work the farms. Decades of rural depopulation had left the countryside desperately short of the manpower needed. Although farm work was a reserved occupation for those over twenty-one, the rural workforce was depleted further when those who had joined the Territorial Army were called up. In 1941, when the reserved occupation age was raised to twenty-five, a further 10,000 countrymen left for the services.

Land at Lake Troutbeck, Cumbria, last cultivated during the First World War, is ploughed once more for growing oats in December 1940.

Gum-booted Land Army Girls rush to bring in the harvest at a Surrey farm.

First among the 'outsiders' drafted in to replace the missing agricultural workers was the Women's Land Army. It was essentially made up of town girls, often young secretaries and office clerks who wanted to 'do their bit'. To begin with, many farmers and their labourers poured scorn on them, assuming farmwork was too dirty and tough for these young and sometimes glamorous city women. The worst time was usually the first few months when the women were learning new skills such as driving tractors and trimming hedges and adjusting to hard manual labour, long working hours and primitive farm accommodation. Most, however, proved they could do the work as well as any man, a fact farmers grudgingly accepted. By 1944, the Women's Land Army was 80,000-strong and commonly used for even the most brutal farm tasks like pest control. Mobile squads were formed which travelled the countryside by bike. The record holders were four North Wales Land Girls who were reported to have destroyed 35,545 rabbits, 7,689 rats, 1,668 foxes and 1,901 moles between February 1941 and April 1942. The Land Army offered rewarding work but members had to be prepared to meet exacting standards and enjoy little leisure time: Land Girls had just seven days' official leave a year compared with twenty-eight days for the armed forces.

Other newcomers had also arrived, provoking similar suspicion and hostility until they proved their mettle on the land. Among them were thousands of conscientious objectors and POWs (prisoners of war). From the summer of 1941 onwards, Italian POWs were working in the fields in gangs guarded by armed soldiers. To begin with they were housed in camps, but soon 'good conduct' prisoners were allowed to live and work on the farms. German POWs joined them in 1944. There was such a big demand from farmers for the strapping POWs that, in the same year, there were over 50,000 employed as agricultural labourers. The Germans were especially prized for their hard work. The main concern for the farmers was to prevent relationships between the POWs and their daughters – the dark-haired Italians in particular were considered very attractive by local girls and romance did blossom, despite the reaction of disapproving parents.

Italian prisoners of war work on the land under the supervision of an armed guard in September 1941.

The massive increase in food production was all the more extraordinary given the loss of three quarters of a million valuable acres to aerodromes, munitions factories, army camps and other British military establishments. Sometimes the best land was taken, as in April 1943, when a huge tract of the East Riding of Yorkshire was commandeered, affecting nearly 10,000 people and 50,000 head of livestock. Whole villages were cleared out, often at very short notice. In the late autumn of 1943, the villagers of Tyneham and Worbarrow in Dorset had to leave their homes when the tank range at Lulworth was extended in preparation for D-Day. They were never allowed back. As D-Day approached, much of rural England was transformed into an army camp. In November 1943 thirty-five square miles of Devon were requisitioned leading to the evacuation of 3,000 villagers and 200 farmers, most of them with only a few weeks' notice. The entry of the United States into the war and the profusion of American military bases in Britain for thousands of GIs swallowed up large tracts of rural Britain. By early 1944, a staggering three million acres of England, Wales and Northern Ireland, around one-thirteenth of their combined land area, had been set aside for the training of the American forces.

Mourners watch as twenty-nine bodies, victims of the bombing of Petworth village school in Sussex, are laid to rest in a communal grave in 1942.

Living cheek by jowl with the military brought danger to the locals who remained. One of the worst disasters of all occurred in the tiny settlement of Frecklington in Lancashire. An American B-24, attempting to land at the nearby American air base, overshot the runway and crashed into the village school. The death toll was horrific. Thirty-eight children and nine adults died. Fatal accidents involving individuals, many of them censored at the time, were commonplace. Some of those especially vulnerable were the farmers and their families who lived adjacent to army training areas. Marjorie Riddaway and her family had a farm in Devon, near to where troops regularly trained with live ammunition:

'Several trench mortar bombs dropped out of aim. We got frightened so my husband went to the army authorities and said, "If you want the farm to train on we'll go because we don't want any casualties." They said it wouldn't be necessary. One day we heard a terrible explosion extremely near our house. John, my son, hadn't come in for dinner but there was nothing unusual about that because he was so conscientious with his work he would stop and finish a job. But as time went by I sent my other son out to look for him. Eventually he came in and said, "Mum, they killed him." The bomb had hit him. I said, "Not my lovely John." He was so happy, so content with life. My heart broke. I lost three stone in about six weeks through the shock.'

Marjorie Riddaway's son John who was killed by 'friendly fire' in 1942.

It was in an atmosphere of war weariness that country people in the rural south-east had to face one final terror: attacks by secret weapons developed by the German high command to undermine civilian morale. It began early in the summer of 1944 with the V1s, or 'doodlebugs', pilotless planes designed to explode on impact, hurled from catapult bases in northern France. Then in November 1945, began another similar assault, this time by V2s, or rockets. All were directed at London but many missed their target and fell – or were shot down – in what came to be called 'doodlebug alley'. The most vulnerable county was Kent. Around 1,500 flying bombs fell there alone, injuring 1,716 people and killing 152 during the last year of the war.

When the war in Europe ended in April 1945, relieved villagers rejoiced. Bonfires were lit, bunting and flags were hung out and there was jubilant dancing on the village green. The villages had formed the forgotten front line on the home front. The countryside had made a major contribution to a nation at war. In doing so it had changed and was a very different place from that of 1939. Town and country had been brought closer together and there was a new interest in productivity and mechanization on the farms. These trends would sow the seeds for the social revolution that would sweep through the countryside during the post-war years.

Sybil Marshall

Sybil Marshall was born in 1913 in the remote village of Ramsey Heights in Huntingdon-shire. After training as a teacher, she went on to pioneer alternative, child-centred teaching methods with an emphasis on art and music. Sybil is now a well known author.

The first weekend of war I was one of those sent to receive the evacuees arriving at Huntingdon station. Children of about six or seven stood shattered and demoralized. They'd all wet themselves. They'd come in on old rolling stock which had no corridors so there were no lavatories available to them. The actual floors of the carriages were in the most filthy mess, they were paddling in it. There were weeping mothers with babies.

I remember clasping to my bosom baby after baby, with everything trickling from its nappy down my front and on to my shoes. We got so used to it we didn't care. The next lot to come off were pregnant mothers, some of them giving birth as we got them out. We had to have medical staff. It was quite indescribable. There was always a train waiting to come in after this one had gone and it never let up for four days.

The poor kids coming out didn't know what was happening. Half were so weary and above everything else, hungry. Many were crying but they were hopeless tears, they weren't making a noise, the tears just dropped off their faces. We were absolutely knocked out ourselves by the sight of them. We didn't know what to expect because we didn't know anything about slumland London, any more than they knew about isolated Huntingdon. The mothers seemed to think that they were going to hotels instead of being pushed into some tiny house in a village.

Some villagers, of course, said they wouldn't have them and ARP (Air Raid Precautions) officers had to tell them that they jolly well had to have them, that this was a war that encompassed everyone. But on the other hand, when you realize that a tiny farm labourer's cottage was the woman's pride and joy to keep as clean and sparkling and as bright as she could, when she found that her two little evacuees wouldn't use the lavatory at all because it was a big hole over a vault and they would go and squat over the fireplace, I don't wonder at her reaction. Country and city people were strangers to one another. It was an enormous experiment to have to take on when one looks back on it.

When the bombing became very bad we had mothers with children in our own house and that was very difficult. On one occasion there was an awful row because our house hadn't any running water and when one of the three husbands came down he made a frightful fuss that his wife and children had been put in a house where there was no running water. My mum said, 'Well, as far as I can see you don't know what it's for anyway,' and she picked up a great big besom brush and started to brush him off the path. In the end we left the house and the evacuees were in by themselves and they wrecked it. They didn't know what a curtain was for. They cut the material off at windowsill level and used it for dish cloths. There wasn't a bed in the house you could have put a pig in, they were so filthy. They burned everything that was burnable; they sawed off the end of a bed to provide them with some warmth because coal was by this time rationed. There wasn't a chair left. They had a party in which they wrecked our ancestral grandfather clock by taking the pendulum and winding it all around the works. My poor old mum and dad had to start all over again. I'm sure they didn't equate the houses they were coming into with people's homes.

By 1940, I was pregnant by my first husband and living with my parents. One day, I was at the breakfast table and was looking out of the window down into the garden which had fruit trees in it and led on to an eight-acre grass field. As I sat watching I saw a Wellington bomber which looked as though it wasn't going to clear our trees, and it went a little bit off-course. When it came into my view again I could actually see the pilot fighting the controls to bring it down somewhere in the flat fields. The next minute, I shall never forget it, there were the awful orange flames of a plane on fire as it crashed and then the filthy dark black smoke which rose from it. By this time my dad had jumped up from his corner of the table and started to run to the plane. One of the men ran up to my brother Gerald and said, 'Shoot me! Shoot me!' He was flaming from head to foot. There were seven men and they burnt to death in my sight. The shock was absolutely terrible to me. I was told after by the doctor that it was seeing them die that caused my baby to turn inside me.

Three months afterwards I went into labour. I stood by my bedroom window with a candle and watched the planes, which had been practising night flying coming in to the aerodrome. A German plane had followed them in and somehow kept out of sight 'til he'd got to the aerodrome. He dropped his stick of bombs with full force. We got the last four just over the border from the farm. I became terribly, terribly ill. It was dark outside, we had no light except candles or an oil lamp, no way of getting messages out to the village. My brother went on his motorbike to fetch the village nurse and finally we got the doctor. The baby was discovered to be in the breech position. The labour went on for three days. The doctor tried desperately to find a place in hospital but every one was packed with wounded men from Dunkirk.

On Sunday morning the doctor said, 'I'm afraid we've got to give you some help.' He spread across my face a piece of cotton and sprinkled chloroform on it. I came

Sybil Marshall (top right) and her class of children in Kingston village school, Cambridgeshire.

round about nine o'clock with him hanging over me saying, 'I've got some very sad news for you.' The baby was stillborn. The doctor had searched all night to find some way he could do a Caesarean but there was nowhere, only my room with a candle and an oil lamp to do it by and no hot water. I called my son William Gregory. He was born on 9 June and I cannot get by that date without starting the day in tears.

In 1942, the new wave of evacuees started. I found myself the only teacher in a village school in Kingston. There was absolutely nothing, just four walls and two cupboards. I had a very mixed lot of thirty-one children, all ages, many evacuees. A lot were so apathetic they hadn't got any life left in them to be naughty, they were just like lumps of clay. I wondered what on earth I was going to do with them.

One day there was a noise outside and in the end I couldn't bear my own curiosity. It was an older Victorian school where the windows were too high to see out of. I hopped on to my high chair but still couldn't see out of the wretched windows so I climbed on my desk. I looked down and the children's mouths were wide open, wondering what on earth this mad woman was doing. It was only a military convoy but then I thought, 'Well, anything's better than nothing,' so I said, 'Hop up on your own desks.' But they couldn't see anything as the windows were so high so I said, 'Well, let's go out and watch it.'

It was at that moment I realized I'd got to use the environment. I thought, 'Oh, let's shut the school door and enjoy what's outside.' We looked at trees which they'd seen hundreds of times before but never really looked at. I remember one little girl actually running her nose up the cracks in the bark of a tree with her arms around it, exploring it with her tongue. At least a quarter of the children were evacuees. Some had only just come, some had been there some time. They didn't really know anything about the countryside, they were terrified of it. The cow is a formidable animal and I could see how they would shrink away if we saw any. The city child thought milk just came in bottles to the doorstep. So I took them to a farm sale where there were cows. The children wanted to run away so I went up to one cow, stroked her, rubbed her between the horns and finally held her muzzle in my hands and kissed her. It made the kids realize they had no more reason to be afraid of cows than they had of a cat, they were part of domestic life in the country. Little by little they learnt things like that without me having to say anything.

The farmers were very good. One day, one said, 'I've got something to show you all but you must be quiet.' We went down to the brook that ran through his land and there was a long-tailed tit's nest and they'd just come out and were sitting along the branch, thirteen of them. The excitement that caused, creeping along the brook! I took them to fields where we made daisy chains and taught them to count by putting them in a chain. I sat down while they dressed me up with them. I must say even the village got a bit worried they had got a mad woman for a teacher when I would walk back to the school trailing daisy chains and crowned with them. I think this was the first time the children *had ever really felt the teachers to be human. It was unusual for a child ever to touch a teacher but they knew I wasn't going to turn on or smack them. It was difficult to have to deal with evacuees, children still missing their own homes very badly and not getting from the people with whom they were billetted the kind of love they needed. I felt it was important to give attention to what I would call the spiritual part of education. I was quite conscious I was teaching the kind of discipline that comes from inside. No-one could fault my children for discipline, they were too anxious to please me.*

Evacuees from the East End of London on a farm in 1941.

John Smith

John Smith was born in Ireland in 1914 to a farming family. He moved to England in 1935 and worked as a gardener on a country estate in Mayfield, Sussex. During the Second World War, John was a farm labourer and member of the Home Guard.

We didn't take much notice of the air-raid siren because it went off all day. You'd never have got anything done on the land, otherwise, so we used to take a hay wagon to shelter under in case. Every now and again I'd switch off the tractor because the engine was so noisy you wouldn't hear the siren.

It was a drizzly but bright and warm day when it happened. Me and Frank, who I'd known for a long time, were in the fields getting ready to cut the tall grass for haymaking. We heard the air-raid siren at Heathfield village about six miles away and the fighter planes in the air. Frank turned to me and said, 'Another robot, John.' Up in the clear skies was a doodlebug. It made a humming noise like a motorbike but much, much louder and there was a six- to eight-foot blue flame coming out from a pipe. We stood in amazement and then it went silent and was pointing towards us. It came down in a straight line and we ran. I dived on the ground and pulled my leather jerkin over my head. The bomb hit the side of a big, green oak tree standing in a dirty swamp and buried itself in a muddy ditch. I waited about five seconds and then it exploded. Mud and sticks flew into the air.

I lay on the ground absolutely dazed. As I got up to look for Frank it was chaos. There was debris everywhere. The blast had hit the stables and there were horses running about. The oak tree was badly scorched and there were great chunks of metal in it. Frank had run to the tree for shelter and I found him lying by the bomb crater. His clothes were blown off him and he was very badly mutilated. It was very gruesome, a dreadful sight. My wife and children were living in the cottage about ten yards away and I rushed to see they were all right. The cottage was a mess: the roof

A shepherd and his flock pass a wrecked German aircraft brought down near the south coast on 7 September 1940.

was completely off, the windows blown out, the end of the house had been pushed from the side walls and there was glass everywhere. The pram had a great big piece of metal in it. I shouted out and found my family upstairs. There were bits of plaster and glass everywhere. Two of the children had taken cover under the bed and my wife and other children were on the bed under the bedclothes. Fortunately no-one was harmed.

It was a real nightmare from beginning to end. I hated the Germans that night. I was shocked and upset and the memory of Frank played on my mind. I couldn't work the next day. The farmer knew we'd been blown up but he gave me the sack for not turning up.

Hilda Cripps

Born in 1909, Hilda Cripps lived in the village of Great Wakering near Southend in Essex with her husband and young daughter during the Second World War. She contributed in many ways to the war effort, firstly as a billeting officer for evacuated children and then as a salvage steward collecting metal from villagers. In 1940 she was sought out to become a member of a secret unit of eight people formed to help villagers in the event of invasion.

One evening after the fall of France the chairman of the parish council came to see me with a letter. He said, 'I can't show the letter to you but I have been told I must set up an invasion committee.' We were near the Thames estuary and close to the Shoeburyness garrison so we were vulnerable. He wanted me to become a member of the committee and although we were never made to swear an oath – there wasn't time – we had to keep our work secret from everyone.

The commander from Shoeburyness garrison visited and told us everything he said was top secret. He said, 'In the event of invasion, which appears to be almost imminent, we shall have to fight over and around you. I want you to bring in all the people from outlying farms into the village. Your main purpose will be to do your best to keep a semblance of normal life going and keep morale up.' He said that any plans that we made, we had to be sure that they didn't include using the roads as these would all be kept strictly for military purposes. Well, we'd seen the newspaper pictures in Holland of people who fled and blocked the roads so their military couldn't use them, so we were well aware of the importance of not doing that.

We expected saturation bombing before the Germans landed so the first thing the committee did was take possession of 420 papier-mâché coffins which we stashed away. We also placed big containers with what was called 'iron rations', which meant basic foods, in various places in the village which could be got to through field paths or people's gardens. We did a census of all livestock and decided in what order the sheep, pigs, hens should be slaughtered. We allocated one large detached house at the top of the village as a hospital in our plans. Another smaller one was to be an isolation hospital. We also knocked on people's doors to find out who the inhabitants were inside them so if their houses were demolished we'd know who we were looking for. No-one ever queried why we were asking them these questions, it was incredible. My own individual job was to take responsibility for the water supply so that if the mains was destroyed we had water. I went to an elderly gentleman in the village, who was a builder, to ask him for houses in the village with wells and he gave me a large list. I went to the Southend water company to get them to inspect which of the wells were fit for drinking or washing and I found out what the capacity was of each so we could work out roughly what the allocation was for each person. It was all done in a very discreet way and no-one ever asked me why I was doing it.

Invasion was being talked about on the wireless all the time. From our back window I could see the bridge to Foulness Island, which is where the invasion of the troops would have come. It was summer time and I used to get up early and look over while it was still misty, half expecting to see troops coming over. My husband and I talked about invasion all the time. We spent a lot of time praying, asking what the right thing to do would be for our little daughter. I didn't worry about what would happen to me but the trauma for a child would have been so great. I kept a bottle of 100 aspirins and if the invasion had started I would have dissolved them in milk and given them to my little girl so she wouldn't wake up. It just seemed the kindest thing to do.

Audrey Witta

At the beginning of the war Audrey Witta was living in London and spent weekends as a volunteer fire-watcher. Born in 1920, she joined the Land Army at the end of 1940.

I was absolutely determined I was going to work on the land. I wanted an open-air life. I went to Victoria Street in London to volunteer for the Land Army and there was an old dear in ghillie shoes [tongueless shoes with lacing up the instep], a real county costume, who measured me. She said, 'Oh dear, I can't take you, you're only four foot eleven and three quarters, we can't take anyone under five feet.' I said, 'If you don't take me I'm not going to do anything.' So she added an extra quarter of an inch to my form. I took a size three shoe but she said there was nothing under a five, so I stomped about for four and a half years in shoes two sizes too big. I told her my waist and bust were four inches bigger than they were because I thought she wouldn't let me in if there was no uniform my size. The clothes swamped me. My mother said I looked like a frog under a dock leaf.

My first post was with my friend Peggy who I'd been working with at Harrods. We were put on a train for Norfolk which stopped in the middle of nowhere and we had to be lifted down because there was no platform. A waiting car took us out to a beautiful old farmhouse. We had to get up the next morning at five o'clock. One of the first jobs we did that day was cleaning the pigsty which hadn't been cleaned for about six months. I said to Peggy, 'I'll go and get our gas masks, that's the best thing.' But she hadn't put soap on hers so when she put it on her face it clouded up. She was supposed to get the fork and rake the muck up and throw it at my feet. Instead she threw it straight at me. I was covered in green slime. The smell, oh dear! It was all in my hair. They had to undress me in the yard. Peggy had some Californian Poppy perfume which she poured all over me. It stunk even worse. Washing had to be done in cold water from the pump. I had to swing on it for Peggy and she swung on it for me. Oh, it was funny.

Land Army Girls gather the rewards of their hard labour at harvest time on a farm in Bury St. Edmunds.

There were just a few decrepit farm labourers and a boy of sixteen. The two older men thought we were silly girls from London. They used to call us a couple of Land Army tarts. But, oh no, we proved our worth. They even used to let us sit in the field with them having thick tea from a big black kettle, wads of bread and cheese and jam. Harvesting always sounds very romantic but it was jolly hard work. When we were bringing in the harvest we worked 'til dark at nearly eleven o'clock at night. We were trying to bring it in quickly to stop the Germans setting it alight because they were dropping incendiary bombs. In the morning, the soldiers used to come round and pick up the ones that hadn't gone off before we could go out with the horses and carts to bring in the stooks.

We were in the thick of it in the country because we'd got air force stations near us everywhere we worked. When we moved down to Walton-on-Thames in Surrey we were given tin hats to wear. We were right in the line for the flying bombs. But these blooming tin hats used to slip down your face and bash you on the nose every time you bent down. We used to hang them and our gas masks in rows on the trees. We were near Hillingdon as well where there was a big American Air Force base where they all went out from for D-Day. I can see the sky now, so thick with these planes you couldn't get a pin between them. We were all waving to the chaps because they were only a few hundred feet above us. The boss kept saying, 'Bend yer backs, you girls,' but we weren't taking a blind bit of notice. After, there was a terrible silence and they started coming back in ones and twos. There was one which was struggling and looked like it was going to crash. We all stopped working to see it but it made it. We were in tears and I think our prayers kept him up there. Then we saw the Red Cross trains coming through. The walking wounded inside were throwing out bits of paper with their names and address on it for us to post to their loved ones. There were some German prisoners of war on the back, looking very surly. We were shouting out, 'You shouldn't have joined up!' and gave them the Victory sign, only it wasn't the Victory sign.

I was with my boy-friend, Eric, for seven years. I'd known him since he was fifteen because we were at school together. Every day I wrote to him and every day he wrote to me. We were only allowed leave for one week of the year in the Land Army, so if I knew he was coming on leave I used to pretend to have a bilious attack so I could see him. All the girls did it for their husbands and boy-friends. The last time I saw Eric he told me, 'Don't mourn for me because you'll find somebody else.' It really upset me. Some time later I had a premonition. I went to work on the Saturday and said to my friend, 'I think Eric was killed last night.' I saw it happen. I'd seen the plane crash and bodies tied up in tarpaulin with ropes around it. When I got home there was a telegram to say 'Missing in Action'. He was shot down over Germany three weeks before he was due to come home. I felt just empty for six months but I had to carry on working. It definitely made me work harder because I really hated the Germans. I wanted to get my own back.

Dot Stephenson

Dot Stephenson, born in 1929, was the daughter of a trawler skipper and grew up in the Hessle Road fishing community in Hull. When she was ten she was evacuated to rural Lincolnshire.

Evacuee Dot Stephenson and her younger brother.

We knew that there was something in the air. No sooner had we sat down in our classrooms than we had to get up again and march into the assembly hall. All the mothers were there. They had little suitcases and paper parcels and boxes and tins. My mother was crying. The headmistress clapped her hands real sweetly and said, 'Now children, you're all going on a holiday. It's a surprise.' Well, it wasn't a surprise – we was gobsmacked. I said to my mum, 'What's going on?' She said, 'You've got to go away because they are going to bomb us and we don't want you to die.' There was screams, there was kids running every which way and mothers grabbing them. It was chaos.

Eventually they got us on these charabancs but we didn't know where we were going. Even our parents didn't know the exact location, they just knew we were going to Lincoln in the country. I'd never been parted from my mother. All the way there we cried. It wasn't just a sob, it was real heart-breaking crying. When we arrived at the village we were taken into the hall and we were all lined up like prize exhibits. We all had our tags on with our names on, our addresses and our father's and mother's occupation. It took hours, people going up and down the line picking out who took their fancy. Some of the kids had nothing; poor was poor in them days. Eventually this woman came. Well, she was done up like a dish of fish with a lemon on top: lipstick, hat, fur coat, high-heeled shoes. She looked down at me. She seemed to be everlasting, like Mount Everest. I didn't like her from minute one. Her husband was a farmer and I loved him on sight, a real nice chap.

When we got to the house she made me sit on a bench outside the French windows at the back. They were talking about me and I could hear everything that was being said because the windows were open. She was saying, 'I don't suppose she knows what a lavatory is, she will have never had a bath before.' She was complaining about all the scruffy children being sent on. Well, my gall was rising. I was getting really angry so at the finish I stomped in, plonked my little suitcase down and I looked her straight in the eye. 'For your information, Madam,' (because 'Madam' was always what my mother called me when I was being saucy), 'we've got a toilet inside and outside. I have a bath every night.' Her husband stood up for me and said she didn't realize what us children had been through, being dragged away from their parents. When I first got there the farmer's wife showed me this little bedroom with little rosebuds on the walls, a beautiful bed, anybody would have been proud to live in there. But the reality was I wasn't in that room, I was in the attic, with a straw palliasse on the floor. I broke my heart the first night. I'd never seen an owl in my life and one sat on the window ledge and all I could see were these two big eyes – petrified I was.

They put us in this lovely little village school. It wasn't like our school; there was only the two classrooms. But they called us the Vaccies and Scruffies and when you

Evacuees arriving to meet their foster mothers at Redbourne Common in Hertfordshire, in 1939.

went in the playground it was like Moses and the water dividing. There was the village kids at one side and the Scruffies on the other side. There were lots of fights and I got in no end of them. The biggest was with a girl who was picking on my friend Beryl. She was crying and had had enough but this girl kept on and so I just went for her. I was only half her size but I didn't give a damn so I flew at her. She swung me round, punched me in the middle of the back and I smacked my head on the window-sill of the school and split my eye open. What you've got to remember is that these kids were well-fed, farm-fed, and we were little, thin shrimps compared to them. We never had fresh air. Mind you, we gave 'em as good as we got.

I had to do chores after school. When the farmer wasn't there she made me do all the washing-up. I had to sweep the stairs and wash the pantry out. I had to wash the hallway and take the washing down from the line, fold it neatly and put it in a basket. I had to feed the pigs and collect the eggs. The jobs had to be done every day, hail, rain or shine. When I used to finish them I had a few hours to myself and I used to wander on the farm. They had some geese they normally kept in a little paddock at the back of the house. This one day the gate had been left open. They had about eight young ones and, oh, you can imagine these little fluffy goslings running about. I picked one up to cuddle it and it was like a red rag to a bull. The geese flew at me. I was putting the gosling down but this big goose attacked me; its wing hit me and snapped me lower arm like a stick.

I was really cheesed, never got no letters from my mum and I didn't know why. I never got no pocket money and she promised me she would send me some. In the end I decided to run away. I planned my escape. I pinched a bike from a shed and waited until dark before going. There was no signposts to find your way home. Fortunately the farmer used to take me to market and one day he'd said, 'This is the way you go when you go home.' I remembered this and I was on the bike pedalling like hell. Oh, I ached. It felt like days. I must have gone a few miles. All of a sudden I could hear this lorry coming and I thought 'Oh God, they're coming after us.' It frightened me to death so I stopped to move the bike on to the side of the road. It was an army lorry and it stopped. The driver said, 'Where do you think you're going this time of night?' I said, 'I'm going home, to Hull.' Well, he said that wasn't far from the barracks where they were going so he said he would take me.

It was about three in the morning when I got back home. I told my mother all about it, all about the work she made me do and about sleeping upstairs on the palliasse. Mother said, 'Why haven't you written to me?' I said, 'You haven't written to me, I've had no letters.' She said, 'But you've had the pocket money I sent'. I said I hadn't. The old cow back there had been keeping my pocket money as well as the letters. From then on I stayed in Hull. There were frightening parts in the war – terrifying – but in the main, it was an adventure. I didn't care where the bombs dropped, how near, as long as I was with my mum. As far as us children were concerned being torn away from our parents was far worse than going through the Blitz.

– Six –

Paradise Lost

Commuting from a village to an office job miles away became fashionable thanks to cheaper cars and improved country roads and railways.

In the post-war years, there has been a social revolution in the British country-side. The nation's farms have been transformed into a highly-mechanized agribusiness, and many villages have been gentrified by the urban middle classes. They have dramatically changed in character from working communities to commuter dormitories, weekend retreats and retirement centres. A new social division has arisen in the countryside between the established families of farmers and farm workers and the affluent newcomers. Many of those who moved out were inspired by a romantic vision of the countryside as a kind of paradise lost. It seemed to offer a rural retreat of peace and beauty, where they could recharge their emotional batteries and find spiritual contentment.

The myth of a 'merrie England', of beautiful estates, thatched cottages and pastoral harmony has a long history. So, too, has the attraction of the wilderness, 'the call of the wild', much celebrated by the romantic poets. Ideals and myths such as these helped shape the aspirations of the newcomers. Even though the life of the middle classes bore little resemblance to the harsh realities of twentieth-century village life and labour, they were immensely powerful. They helped create a vision of what the countryside should be, a 'green and pleasant land', which the newcomers were prepared to fight for. This was often very different from the world view of modernizing, profit-driven farmers.

The newcomers were often those who had discovered the delights of the countryside as children. The trend for weekend visits into the country began in late Victorian and Edwardian times with the development of cycling and rambling clubs in many industrial towns. But the movement took off during the inter-war years, when many thousands of 'townies' set out to explore the hills, lakes and valleys. The cult of fresh air and country exercise was celebrated in the hit song, 'I'm Happy When I'm Hiking'.

The Rambler's Association was formed in 1932, and immediately launched a campaign to open up the moors and the hills to the public. In April of that year, it helped stage-manage a mass trespass of the Duke of Devonshire's grouse moors at Kinder Scout in the High Peak district of Derbyshire. Five of the leaders were arrested and imprisoned, but the issue of public access to private land had been firmly established. By the late 1930s, more of the countryside was made accessible to the ramblers, who poured out of the cities on special excursions into the villages on summer Saturdays.

More and more city-dwellers saw the countryside as a place of relaxation and leisure after the war.

The real boom in rural tourism came in the post-war years, and behind it lay a huge increase in car ownership. The popularity of motor-car visits to the countryside had begun during the inter-war years, but between 1945 and 1960 car ownership quadrupled. Most of the trips revolved around picnics, visits to ancient monuments or short walks. Country tourism was still relatively unsophisticated and what most people wanted was just a 'view with a loo'. The weekend exodus of city dwellers was further boosted by the opening up of stately homes by the cash-strapped aristocracy. Hit by falling incomes, rising repair costs and death duties, they opened their doors to the general public who now became their cash-paying guests.

Among the pioneers in the early post-war years were, first, Lord Bath at Longleat and then Lord Montagu at Beaulieu in Hampshire. Lord Montagu astutely combined the attractions of motoring and the stately houses by opening Britain's first motor museum. By the 1960s, a host of titled families were cashing in on a nation's nosiness and reverence, offering guided tours around their historic inner sanctums and miniature steam railway rides around their landscaped gardens. Stately homes became the most popular country destination, not only for early motorists but also for weekend coach excursions. They were the jewel in the crown of a growing heritage industry of converted mills, rural museums, period pubs, 'olde worlde' tea shops, antique and craft establishments, preserved steam railways, country footpaths, beauty spots and a host of other attractions.

Increasing numbers of city and suburban dwellers enjoyed the countryside so much that they wanted to live there. Long-distance commuting had begun in the late Victorian era with the development of the railway network and had increased during the inter-war years, especially in the Home Counties. However, it only started to become really fashionable in the post-war years. Again, the key factor was the car, now cheaper, faster and more reliable than ever before, and travelling along rural roads that had been much improved since the early part of the century. Now it was relatively easy to commute directly from a

Opposite
Tourists in Helston in Cornwall watch the all-day dancing during Flora Day celebrations in May 1952. There was a big revival of folk customs in the post-war years.

remote village to an office job in a town or city many miles away. The real long-distance travellers usually combined a car and train journey, often parking at station car parks or nearby.

Many villages were ripe for new development, as a result of farm mechanization and local inhabitants leaving the land to look for jobs in the cities. Rural Surrey was the first region to be colonized by London commuters, who turned run-down farming communities into metropolitan villages. This trend spread rapidly throughout the Home Counties and then to more outlying areas. The electrification of Eastern Region lines to Liverpool Street opened up many Essex villages to London commuters in the late 1950s. A decade later, a similar pattern had emerged around most of the major towns and cities all over Britain. Gentrifiers snapped up semi-derelict cottages and farmhouses at bargain prices. New housing developments, often with custom-built detached homes offering double garages for two-car families, sprouted up on the outskirts of villages. It was assumed that the husband would drive to the station while the wife needed her own car to get around the village, do the shopping and take the children to and from school.

The 'pioneer' middle-class families who moved out often had high hopes for their new life in the villages. Escaping from the traffic-choked inner cities and the safe conformity of the suburbs, they were embarking on a great adventure. Many couples wanted a place with 'character' in which to live – and they set about restoring period homes. Their enthusiasm was sometimes dampened as they became aware of the inconveniences and sacrifices of a village life. In the 1950s and early 1960s, many villages were still poorly served by main services such as gas, electricity and sewers. For example, many of the newcomers had to make do with a smelly cesspit in the back garden. Improvements took years and often proved costly. Schools were few and far between, and some became hopelessly overcrowded as the village population boomed.

But what was most hurtful to these families was the fact that they were often viewed with suspicion, or even shunned, by the locals. Many who moved out had shared a romantic ideal that they would be joining a friendly community of rustic villagers. The reality was that the locals frequently resented this colonization by people who were much better off than themselves, and who were turning their village into a 'gin and Jag' belt. The newcomers travelled around by car, breaking down much of the face-to-face daily contact that had been part of the social fabric of the old way of life. The locals saw their pubs changing in character and their parish council taken over by a set of townies with posh voices. Most importantly, they saw the transformation of their village from a working community into a commuter suburb.

Opposite
Agricultural labourers did not share in the post-war prosperity of farming. Their wages remained some of the lowest in Britain.

Gentrification spread in the 1970s and 1980s as many villages in counties such as Oxfordshire, Gloucestershire and Wiltshire became commuter outposts. The establishment of a national motorway network meant that remote villages and hamlets all over Britain had the potential for gentrification. The boom in house prices in the cities provided an added incentive to move out and take advantage of cheap cottages and generous government improvement grants. The middle-class newcomers were now in the ascendant and they restored their homes with a loving attention to detail. There were thatched roofs, oak beams and cottage gardens aplenty, and the villages had probably never looked more beautiful. The newcomers had successfully turned the countryside into a rustic retreat, halting generations of decline in the villages.

The new villagers formed the backbone of the conservation movement. They had a picturesque and unchanging image of what the countryside should be like and they began a battle to keep it quintessentially rural. They were affluent and articulate, unlike the older generation of villagers who were often deferential. The concern to conserve the British countryside and its historic buildings was not new, however. The National Trust was formed in 1895 and had grown rapidly in the number of its properties and influence. The Council for the Preservation of Rural England, founded in 1926, helped form a recognizable environmental lobby with its inter-war defence of the countryside against urban sprawl, ugly electricity pylons and advertizing hoardings. The conservation movement won a series of major victories in the late 1940s with legislation that created green belts around the cities, and national parks protecting areas of outstanding beauty from development. The gentrifiers used existing laws to oppose in their villages any new building which might spoil their rustic charm.

But this growing colonization and conservation created new social problems in the villages. As gentrifiers wanted to keep their picturesque villages preserved in aspic, they generally opposed the building of cheap homes or council houses that might have accommodated the rural working classes. At the same time, the price of cottages went up so much that the sons and daughters of local families could no longer afford to live in their home villages. The newcomers often used their cars to shop and socialize outside the village. As a result, there was often less demand for village shops, post offices and public transport services, many of which were lost. In most villages the conflict remained simmering beneath the surface, but in West Wales it took a dramatic twist when, in the 1970s, militant Welsh nationalists began setting fire to the second homes of the English newcomers who had begun to colonize the coastal villages.

However, the main conflict involving the new villagers was farming. The unspoilt, timeless English countryside was changing fast. After the war,

agriculture was transformed into an agri-business, continuing the trend begun during the Second World War. The thrust of modern agriculture was towards bigger, prairie-style farms that were highly capitalized. Many small family farms went out of business and were replaced by a new breed of agribusinessmen, farming thousands of acres. In ten years, horses almost disappeared from the land as farming became a highly-mechanized system of production involving tractors and sophisticated combine harvesters. By the late 1960s, the harvest which had once taken weeks to gather, was completed in days. There were far fewer jobs on the land and the number of farm labourers shrunk from around three quarters of a million in 1949 to a quarter of a million thirty years later.

Weedkiller is sprayed onto a thirty-acre field of barley in 1966 in Farmington, Gloucestershire. Intensive use of chemicals epitomized modern agriculture.

By the 1960s and 1970s, this new system made British agriculture one of the most efficient and profitable in the world. Crop yields leapt almost every year. Productivity was boosted by artificial fertilizers and the widespread use of pesticides. Plant and animal breeding made huge advances. Assembly-line methods were applied to animals in the new factory farms, which came to dominate the production of cheap meat and eggs. The whole system was backed by the government, the aim being a prosperous farming industry and the production of not only more but cheaper food as well. It was embodied in the Agriculture Act of 1947 which guaranteed fixed prices and generous subsidies for farmers. All this was paid for by the taxpayer, provoking accusations of 'feather bedding'. But by the late 1960s, the farmers, who before the war had been celebrated as the custodians of our rural heritage, were now facing the more serious charge that in their search for greater profits, they were destroying everything that was most cherished about the countryside.

While the village newcomers were able to use planning laws to restrict new building in their area, they discovered that agriculture remained, for the most part, exempt from planning legislation. This became a major cause for concern. A new movement to control modern farming methods was sparked by the book, *Silent Spring*, written in 1962 by the American scientist, Rachel Carson. She was the first to point out that the indiscriminate use of chemical pesticides such as D.D.T., widely used in Britain during the 1940s and 1950s, was having a devastating effect on wildlife and was undermining the ecological balance of the countryside. Equally alarming, toxic substances were passing into the human food chain. By the 1970s, the protection of the environment had become a national political issue.

A tree is removed from a Sussex farm. Thousands of miles of hedgerows were ripped up in the post-war years to make way for new prairie-style farms.

One of the greatest controversies was the disappearance of hedgerows. Mechanization had made them redundant and they were cut down to make way for a featureless prairie, ideal for modern cereal farming with combine harvesters. In Norfolk, for example, 8,500 miles of hedges, almost half of the county's hedgerows, were removed between 1946 and 1970. These hedgerows, quite apart from their beauty, provided an important habitat for many species of plants and wildlife, and often had historic significance in marking the boundaries of parishes or estates.

Many other landscape features were removed in the rush to profit from the booming agribusiness. Woodlands were bulldozed, ponds filled in, heaths and moorlands ploughed up, wetlands drained, all giving the countryside an ordered, uniform appearance and robbing it of local diversity and colour. There was a direct conflict of interest between the new farmers, who viewed the countryside principally as a source of profit, and the conservationists, who viewed it as a source of visual pleasure and enjoyment. The conservationists also cared much more passionately about the possible damaging effects of modern farming methods on wildlife and the ecological system. By the early 1980s, there were fewer than 200,000 farmers in the country but conservation groups had a membership of more than two million. The weight of public opinion, demanding an end to the most destructive farming methods and a preservation of Britain's rural heritage, was reflected in the growing intervention of the new Department of the Environment. Some of the worst acts of rural vandalism by agribusinessmen were ended.

As the new millennium dawns, the British countryside has become a political arena in a way inconceivable to previous generations. Agenda-led councils and newcomers to rural life clamour to have their say. Environmental groups such as Friends of the Earth and the new eco warriors have become increasingly vociferous in their protests against countryside pollution. Leisure organizations such as the Rambler's Association have never seen membership so high and demand, with increasing success, the right to roam huge tracts of countryside to which landowners still oppose public access. In recent years, farmers have been pushed back on to the defensive. The waste of taxpayers' money on the production of food mountains and the regular food panics like the BSE crisis all put a question mark over modern farming methods. Some of the government support on which the farmers have become so dependent has been withdrawn. State bureaucracy has increased with the added complication of EU regulations and the Common Agricultural Policy. Even fox hunting, a traditional sport beloved by old-established farming families and landowners, has been branded barbaric and now faces a ban. The future of the countryside and how it should be used today, are matters of fierce debate.

Car ownership quadrupled between 1945 and 1960 and weekend drives to charming country pubs like this one in Denham, Buckinghamshire became very popular.

All this is a far cry from the rural Britain of the first decades of the century, when the issues were much clearer. For most people, country life was simply a matter of survival. The old world characterized by child labour on the land, large estates that controlled the local population and small farmers using traditional horse and hand methods has all become a distant memory.

One of the few features of rural life that has remained more or less constant throughout the century is the low pay and poor working conditions of the farm labourers. Very little of the prosperity of post-war farming has been passed on to them. In recent decades, they have had to face the double blow of rising rural unemployment and the decline of cheap rural housing. Farm labourers began and ended the twentieth century as having one of the lowest-paid occupations in Britain.

Further Reading

Alan Armstrong, *Farmworkers: A Social and Economic History* (Batsford, London, 1988)

Anthony Barnett and Roger Scruton, *Town and Country* (Jonathan Cape, London, 1998)

Phyllida Barstow, *The English Country House Party* (Thorsons, London, 1989)

J.H. Betty, *Estates and the English Countryside* (Batsford, London, 1993)

Ronald Blythe, *Akenfield* (Penguin, London, 1972)

Georgina Boyes, *The Imagined Village* (Manchester University Press, Manchester, 1993)

Angus Calder, *The People's War* (Pimlico, London, 1997)

David Cannadine, *Decline and Fall of the British Aristocracy* (Yale University Press, London, 1990)

Frank Victor Dawes, *Not in Front of the Servants* (Hutchinson, London, 1984)

George Ewart Evans, *Where Beards Wag All* (Faber and Faber, London, 1970)

Graham Harvey, *The Killing of the Countryside* (Vintage, London, 1998)

Pamela Horn, *The Changing Countryside* (Athlone Press, London, 1984)

Pamela Horn, *Rural Life in England in the First World War* (Gill & Macmillan, Dublin, 1984)

Pamela Horn, *The Victorian Country Child* (Sutton Publishing, Stroud, 1998)

Pamela Horn, *Women in the 1920s* (Sutton Publishing, Stroud, 1995)

Alun Howkins, *Poor Labouring Men* (Routledge, London, 1985)

Alun Howkins, *Reshaping Rural England* (HarperCollins, London, 1991)

Steve Humphries and Pamela Gordon, *A Labour of Love* (Sidgwick & Jackson, London, 1993)

Steve Humphries, *A Secret World of Sex* (Sidgwick & Jackson, London, 1991)

Charles Kightly, *Country Voices* (Thames and Hudson, London, 1984)

Howard Newby, *Country Life: A Social History of Rural England* (Sphere, London, 1988)

Howard Newby, *The Countryside in Question* (Hutchinson, London, 1988)

Robin Page, *Vocal Yokel* (Excellent Press, London, 1996)

Raphael Samuel, *Village Life and Labour* (Routledge, London, 1975)

Roy Strong, *Country Life 1897–1997 The English Arcadia* (Boxtree, London, 1996)

Sadie Ward, *War in the Countryside* (Cameron, London, 1988)

Sadie Ward and John Creasey, *The Countryside Between the Wars* (Batsford, London, 1984)

Raymond Williams, *The Country and the City* (Chatto & Windus, 1973)

S. B. Smith, *The Retreat of Tuberculosis 1850–1950* (Croom Helm, London, 1988)

Index